MBA in 2 Weeks

SANDEEP GOYAL

MBA, University of Texas at Austin
MSEE, University of Calgary

Disclaimer: While the publisher and author have used their best efforts in preparing this book, they make no representations or warranties with respect to the accuracy and completeness of the contents of this book. The publisher and author are not engaged in rendering legal, accounting, financial, or any other professional services, and the reader should consult with a professional where appropriate. Neither the publisher nor author shall be liable for any damages, including but not limited to loss of profit, commercial damage, special, incidental, consequential and/or other damages.

Copyright © 2016 Sandeep Goyal

All rights reserved.

ISBN-10: **1523475196**
ISBN-13: **978-1523475193**

Preface

This book contains all the key business and management educational topics taught in the top MBA programs. It provides the most important and useful MBA learning material in a very simple and easy to understand language.

It allows anyone who wants to learn these skills to be able to quickly understand key business concepts and apply in their everyday life, and recognize the application of these concepts – be it inflation, stock earning reports, business loans, management tactics, or advertising etc. The topics are limited to the most important ones, and complex concepts are explained in a plain and easy to follow way.

Why learn MBA concepts? When somebody thinks of an MBA program, one of the first things that come to mind is that it will help get a higher salary job. But learning MBA concepts is much more than that. This knowledge can help small business owners run their operations more efficiently and also make better decisions regarding pricing, volume production etc.

to improve their profitability, it helps product managers design their new products much better as per customer needs and launch them on time, it helps managers learn motivational techniques and improve employee productivity, it helps individual investors learn how to properly analyze financial statements and make better investment decisions and much more ....

To family and friends

CONTENTS

Day 1 and 2	Economics	1
Day 3 and 4	Financial Accounting	19
Day 5	Managerial Accounting	41
Day 6 and 7	Operations Management	55
Day 8, 9, and 10	Finance	73
Day 11 and 12	Marketing	113
Day 13	Strategic Management	129
Day 14	Organizational Behavior	147

Recommended Readings   *161*

ECONOMICS

Introduction

The fundamental issue that the study of Economics tries to deal with is that of "Scarcity". Simply put, we human beings have unlimited wants and needs, but there are only limited resources. Economics tries to understand this tension and studies how this can be done with maximum efficiency. Macroeconomics takes a top down approach and looks at the issue from very high level – national level, whereas Microeconomics takes bottom-up approach and looks from the level of an individual or a firm. Demand and supply are fundamental to Economics, so it is important to understand their characteristics and relationship with price.

Topics in Brief

Demand: Demand refers to how much quantity of a good (product or service) people want to get. This quantity is dependent upon the price of that given good. *"Law of Demand"* is an economic law that states that people buy more of a good as the price goes down, and buy less if price goes up.

Supply: Supply refers to the quantity or amount of a good that the producers are willing and able to sell at a given price. Just like Demand, this amount is dependent upon the price and governed by the "Law of Supply". Unlike Demand, however, Supply increases with the increase in price, and vice versa.

Equilibrium: Market is said to be in Equilibrium when the Price is such that the Quantity of goods is same from both the Demand side and the Supply side.

Elasticity: Elasticity is defined as Change in Quantity per unit Change in Price. This is true for both Demand and Supply Elasticity.

Opportunity Cost: This is another important concept in Economics and ties back to the problem of "Scarcity" – unlimited needs and wants, and limited resources. It is defined as the value of the next best alternative use (which was not chosen) of that resource.

Macroeconomics Basics: Gross Domestic Product (GDP) and Gross National Product (GNP).

Multiplier Effect: For every dollar of initial deposit or government spending, the effect on overall economy is much higher due to the multiplier effect, and depends upon Bank Reserve Ratio and consumer Marginal Propensity to Consume

Inflation: Inflation is increase in general level of prices of goods and services. Over time, due to inflation, a person will be able to buy fewer goods and services for the same amount of money.

Demand

Demand refers to how much quantity of a good (product or service) people want to get. This quantity is dependent upon the price of that given good.

"Law of Demand" is an economic law that states that people buy more of a good as the price goes down, and buy less if price goes up. It can be summarized in a very popular graph:

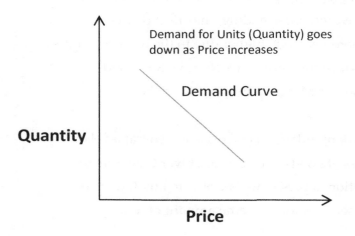

As the price goes up or down (on the horizontal axis), the demand goes down as per the demand curve. It should be noted that movement along the demand curve happens only upon any price changes. Other changes, such as change in the number of customer demographics, cause a shift in the demand curve.

Demand Curve Shift: Consider a case when the overall demand increases due to an increase in the population. This change in demand causes a shift in the demand curve towards the right. Similarly, a decrease in demand will cause a leftward shift in the

demand curve. Some of the common causes for demand shift are:
- Population/demographics change
- Change in income levels
- Change in taste/values/preferences
- Arrival in market of other goods that can serve as substitute
- Change in prices of complement or substitute goods
- Anticipation or expectation of future price change

Supply

Supply refers to the quantity or amount of a good that the producers are willing and able to sell at a given price. Just like Demand, this amount is dependent upon the price and governed by the "Law of Supply". Unlike Demand, however, Supply increases with the increase in price, and vice versa. This happens because if the prices increase, producers want to sell even more quantity of goods to increase the revenue and the profits. The Supply Curve is shown below, and unlike Demand Curve, it has an upward slope:

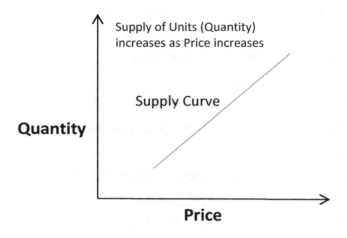

Supply Curve Shift: Just like Demand Curve, Supply Curve also gets shifted due to many reasons (other than price change, which only causes the movement along the Curve). When the Supply increases, the Curve shifts to the left, and when the Supply decreases the curve shifts to the right. Shift is caused by factors that affect the supply:

- Production costs
- Price of inputs
- Production issues (like availability of technology, labor strike, good/bad weather etc.)
- Expectation/anticipation of future price changes
- Competition (number of suppliers in the market)
- Regulatory issues

Equilibrium

Market is said to be in Equilibrium when the Price is such that the Quantity of goods is same from both the Demand side and the Supply side. In other words, producers supply exactly same amount of goods as the consumers want to buy at that given price. It is the point where the Demand Curve intersects the Supply Curve.

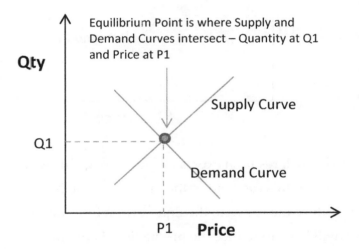

What happens when the market is not in Equilibrium?

Consider the case when the price of a product is set higher than the Equilibrium Price. Although the Suppliers will be producing higher quantity of goods

Q2 (from Supply Curve), but if we look at the Demand Curve, the consumers will buy lesser amount of goods Q1.

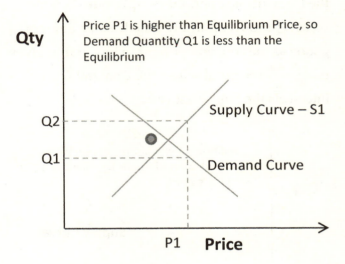

This will result in excess inventory of goods (Q2 – Q1). In this case, either the producers will have to reduce the prices to the Equilibrium Price or they will have to reduce the production. Reducing production will shift the supply curve to the right and a new equilibrium point will be reached.

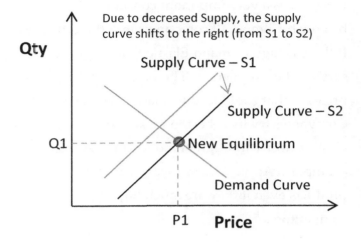

Elasticity

Elasticity is defined as Change in Quantity per unit Change in Price. This is true for both Demand and Supply Elasticity. The more important of the two is Demand Elasticity as this is used in pricing of various goods. If we look at the Demand Curve, Elasticity is measured by the slope of the line (Demand Curve). If the Elasticity is more than one (there is higher change in Quantity for a given change in Price), then that good is said to have Elastic Demand. However, if the Elasticity is less than one (lower change in Quantity for a given change in Price) then the demand is Inelastic.

Elasticity is a very important concept which is used heavily by almost all companies in setting the prices. If there is high Demand Elasticity for a product or service, the suppliers will be very wary of increasing prices as that could lead to a large decline in sales. Companies try their best to make their products less elastic (mostly through brand loyalty). A major example is Apple, whose loyal customers buy Apple products even if they are much higher priced than its competitors.

Another major factor affecting Elasticity is Substitute products. If there are good substitutes available, consumers will buy those in case of a price increase, thus increasing the Elasticity.

Product differentiation or innovation also helps decrease Elasticity. If a company comes up with a product which is highly differentiated and innovative (so it has very few substitutes), Elasticity will decline. However, for products where there is no differentiation at all, Elasticity is very high. Commodity products like Oil, Grains etc. are great examples of products with high Elasticity.

Opportunity Cost

This is another important concept in Economics and ties back to the problem of "Scarcity" – unlimited needs and wants, and limited resources. It is defined as the value of the next best alternative use (which was not chosen) of that resource. In simple terms, Opportunity Cost is what all you give up to obtain something. If you just buy something while in market, it is simply the price you pay. But now consider the case when something is available for $100 in that market and for $90 in a place 20 miles away. If you decide to go there and buy for $90, your opportunity cost would be $90 + cost of gas + car wear and tear + your time (driving back and forth). So you make the purchase decision based upon your estimate of whether this Opportunity Cost is higher or lower than $100 that you can pay to buy on the spot.

MACRO-ECONOMICS

As mentioned earlier, Macro-economics takes a top down approach and looks at issues from national level. While it is a very broad field, this book will discuss only some of the more important issues that are more relevant in normal business circumstances.

GDP stands for Gross Domestic Product, and represents *total value of goods and services produced in a country*. It is commonly viewed as a measure on the size of economy of a country. It is important to note that it also includes goods and services by companies that are owned by foreign nationals or companies. Also, growth in GDP (Year over Year) is a very popular metric to see which countries are growing faster vs. others. If GDP shows negative growth, then a country is believed to be in recession.

The most common method of measuring GDP is using Expenditure Method. Here, GDP is sum of all Public (Consumer) Consumption, Business Investments, Government Spending, and Net Exports (Exports – Imports).

GNP (Gross National Product) is similar to GDP but measures the total value from country ownership perspective, irrespective of location. Let's say there is a factory owned by a US national in Canada. The output of that will be Canadian GDP but US GNP.

Multiplier Effect: Money Supply and GDP Growth

Multiplier Effect is a crucial concept in understanding of macro-economics. This concept underpins many of the actions taken by central banks all over the world. First, you need to understand some more basics:

Banks and Reserve Ratio: Banks generally take deposits from a customer, and then use those deposits to lend money to other customers. However, they are not allowed to lend all of the money, and are required to hold some portion of that in cash. This portion is called Reserve Requirement or Reserve Ratio. Currently, the US Reserve Requirement (for banks with more than $71 Million in net transactions) is 10%.

How Banks Make Money: Banks typically make money by paying lower interest rates for the deposits and lending money at higher rates to its customers.

Marginal Propensity to Save (MPS) and Marginal Propensity to Consume (MPC): These terms refer to the portion of the increased income that the consumers decide to either save or consume. For example, if for every dollar of increased income, consumers spend $0.85 and save the rest $0.15, then:

Marginal Propensity to Save (MPS) = 0.15
Marginal Propensity to Consume (MPC) = 0.85

Normally in a closed economy, MPS + MPC =1

Now, we are ready to discuss the Multiplier Effect.
Money Supply Multiplier Effect: The amount of money supply in an economy is impacted by the Reserve Ratio. Let's say the Reserve Ratio is 0.20 or 20%. A person deposits $100 in a Bank. The Bank will hold 20% of this amount ($20) and lend the remaining $80 to another customer. That customer will deposit this $80 into another Bank, which will set aside 20% of this ($16) and lend the remaining

$64 to another customer, and this cycle goes on. *Can you guess the total amount of money deposited in all the Banks due to that initial $100 deposit?*

A: It is $500.
This can be calculated by
*(Initial Deposit)/(Reserve Ratio) = $100/0.2 = $500
So, the Multiplier is 1/(Reserve Ratio) = 1/0.2 = 5*

Thus, by changing the Reserve Ratio, Central banks can impact the total money supply in an economy. Typically, when economy is weak, they try to stimulate the economy by lowering the Reserve Ratio and increasing the Money Supply. On the other hand, if growth has been very strong and there is fear of inflation, they typically increase the Reserve Ratio to limit the Money Supply in the economy.

Multiplier Effect on GDP or Income: The Multiplier Effect also has impact on GDP or National Income. For every dollar of initial spending (by government or private sector) there is magnified effect on overall economy, depending upon Marginal Propensity to Consume (MPC). For example, a new Building is constructed in a town. The cost is $100 which owners give to a construction company. Let's assume MPC for the companies and consumers is same at 0.90. The construction company saves $10 and spends $90 on raw materials and labor costs. The raw material companies and workers save 10% of what they get and spend 90% of it, and this cycle continues.

The total amount of increase in spending (you can also call it GDP or Income) will be $1,000.
So, the Multiplier is 10 ($1,000/$100).
Formula for Multiplier is: *1/MPS or 1/(1 − MPC)*

This is the reason why governments start investment projects when economy is weak, as it has a magnified impact on the overall economy.

Inflation
Inflation is the increase in general level of prices of goods and services. Thus over time, due to inflation, a person will be able to buy fewer goods and services for the same amount of money.

A little bit of inflation (normally less than 2-3%) is not considered too bad, but if it starts increasing too much, it is considered very worrisome for the economy. Fear of loss of purchasing power discourages savings and investments, and often people end up making irrational investments just to retain the purchasing power, and with bad consequences. Countries with high inflation see their currencies get devalued compared to other currencies, causing reduction in national wealth level.

Causes of Inflation: Causes of inflation could vary according to circumstances and could also be a mix of different factors. Three main causes proposed by economists are:

1) Increase in Money Supply: According to this theory, an increase in Money Supply causes an increase in general price levels, causing inflation.

2) Demand-Pull Inflation: When there is an increase in demand levels that can't be matched by supply, price levels rise and cause inflation.

3) Cost-Push Inflation: Inflation occurs when either there is a decrease in supply levels (could be due to various factors like natural disasters, strikes, disputes etc.) or an in increase in cost levels (due to rising labor costs, higher raw material costs etc.). Suppliers need to increase prices to maintain their profit margins, resulting in inflation.

Controlling Inflation: Nowadays the most common tool for tackling inflation is considered to be Monetary Policy. This is achieved by increasing the interest rates and reducing the growth in Money Supply in the economy.

FINANCIAL ACCOUNTING

Introduction

Financial Accounting is the branch of Accounting that deals with the process of book-keeping and preparation of financial statements according to national and international accounting standards. The purpose is to convey information about a company's financial matters according to common standards for the use by shareholders, prospective investors, government authorities, and others.

Topics in Brief

Financial Statements: There are four major financial statements:

1) Balance Sheet: Balance Sheet contains information about company's assets, liabilities, and ownership equity on a given date

2) Income Statement: Income Statement contains details about Income derived during a period of time. The details include Revenues (sales), various costs (includes Cost of Goods Sold, R&D expense,

Selling/Marketing costs, General & Administrative expenses, Depreciation costs etc.)

3) Cash Flow Statement: Cash Flow Statement looks at actual Cash Flow through a period of time, and records the cash transactions as they occur

4) Statement of Changes in Equity: It shows details of changes in owner's (or shareholders) equity and retained earnings over a period of time

Financial Ratios: There are different types of ratios that provide more insights into a company's financial condition and allow people to compare different companies. Financial ratios are mostly categorized into four major groups:

1) Profitability Ratios: These ratios measure how profitable a firm is compared to metrics like sales, equity, assets etc.

2) Operating Efficiency Ratios: These ratios measure how efficiently a firm is utilizing its assets.

3) Leverage (Debt) Ratios: These ratios measure the relative level of a company's debt and its solvency

4) Liquidity Ratios: These ratios measure a firm's ability to be able to pay its short term obligations.

BALANCE SHEET

Balance Sheet contains information about the company's assets, liabilities, and ownership equity on a given date. It is important to understand that this information is as of the reported date i.e. snapshot at a given time. Let's understand various items contained in a Balance Sheet.

Assets

Assets are basically anything owned by the company like cash, investments, property, land, equipment, raw materials, inventory, patents etc. Assets normally have economic value and are measurable in monetary terms. Assets are further categorized in two groups – Current Assets and Non-current assets.

Current assets are the ones that can be converted to cash within one year. Normal items under current assets include cash, cash equivalents (like money market holdings, marketable securities, T-bills etc.), short-term investments, accounts receivables, inventories etc.

Non-current assets are fixed assets that can't be converted to cash quickly, and typically include property, long-term investments, intangible assets (like patents, copyright etc.), and goodwill.

Inventory: Inventory consists of goods or parts that have been purchased but not sold yet. Inventory is generally of three types – Raw Materials, Work In Progress, and Finished Goods.
Consider an example of a Food Products company. Normally it would buy raw materials like grains, corn, milk, and other agricultural products and then send those to its factories where they are converted to the final products. At the time of Balance Sheet preparation, any products that are still in raw material form are classified as Raw Material inventory, those that are in the process of being converted to final products are Work In progress (WIP) inventory, and finally those who have become final products but not yet sold/shipped to the customers are called Finished Goods inventory.

Property, Plants & Equipment (PP&E): This includes items like Land, Buildings and Machinery owned by the company.

Please Note -Land is calculated at the cost price i.e. if land was bought 15 years ago for $1,000, its value on the Balance Sheet would still show $1,000 even though the market price now may be much higher. For Property and Equipment, the accumulated depreciation is taken out, so the value shown on the Balance Sheet is net of depreciation.

Depreciation Calculation: Usually fixed assets like buildings and machinery/equipment go down in value over time and eventually need replacement. This reduction in value is accounted as Depreciation, and is usually done in a linear method over the useful life of the asset. For example, a company buys a new machine for $1,000 which is expected to last 5 years, and a new building for $500,000 expected to last 20 years. Then the yearly Depreciation will be $200 for the machine ($1,000 divided by 5) and for calculating building depreciation per year, we will divide initial cost of $500,000 by useful life of 20 years = 500,000 / 20 = $25,000 per year. This method is also called Straight Line Depreciation.

Liabilities
Liabilities are obligations that the company needs to pay like loans, notes payable, short-term debt, accounts payable, taxes, long-term debt etc. Liabilities are also further classified into current (due within one year) and non-current liabilities.

<u>Current liabilities</u> typically include short-term debt, current portion of long-term debt, accounts payable, current portion of tax etc.

<u>Non-current liabilities</u> mostly include items like long-term debt, deferred tax liabilities (tax that will be paid in future years), pension obligations, lease obligations etc.

Owner's Equity
The difference between Assets and Liabilities is Owner's Equity. Suppose a company has $100 worth of total assets and $75 in total liabilities. Then, the Owner's Equity is $25 ($100 - $75).

$$\textit{Owner's Equity} = \textit{Assets} - \textit{Liabilities}$$
$$\textit{or}$$
$$\textit{Assets} = \textit{Liabilities} + \textit{Owner's Equity}$$

INCOME STATEMENT

Income Statement, as the name implies, contains details about Income derived <u>during</u> a period of time. The details include Revenues (sales), various costs (includes Cost of Goods Sold, R&D expense, Selling/Marketing costs, General & Administrative expenses, Depreciation costs etc.). Unlike Balance Sheet, which contains snapshot of information at a given point of time, Income Statement is for a period of time (usually a Quarter or a Year).

Income Statement is also known by some other names like Earnings Statement, Revenue Statement, P&L (Profit & Loss) Statement, and Statement of Operations. Let's take a look at a typical Income Statement and definition of its major components:

Revenue — Total money obtained from selling goods & services

Cost of Goods Sold (COGS) — Costs directly related to production of goods. Major components are raw material costs, labor costs (in factories), and production related overhead costs. Also includes depreciation for production related property and equipment.

Gross Margin = Revenue – COGS

Operating Costs:

R&D — Expense related to Research & Development (includes machinery, salary, as well as overhead costs)

Selling/Marketing Expense — Includes costs related to advertising, promotion, sales commission, salaries

	in sales & marketing, overhead etc.
General & Administrative	Expenses to run and maintain the business like office building expense, supplies, administration and support staff salaries etc.
Depreciation/Amortization	Only assets used in operating expenses are depreciated under Operating Expenses. For equipment and buildings used directly for producing goods, depreciation is used in COGS.
Other Operating expenses	Other miscellaneous expenses not covered in any of the above categories

---

Operating Profit = Gross Margin − Operating Expenses
(Also known as EBIT, Earnings Before Interest and Taxes)

Non-operating Costs:

Other Gains	Gains or profits from activities not related to business. Examples include litigation win, gain from sales of securities or an asset etc.
Other Losses	Losses arising from non-business related factors like loss from sale of securities at lower price, foreign exchange loss etc.
Interest Proceeds/Costs	Includes gains from interest received and costs related to payment of interest for debt

----

Profit Before Tax = Operating Profit − Non-operating Costs

(Also known as EBT, Earnings Before Taxes)

Income Tax	Income Tax due on the income generated for the period. Note that this

income tax doesn't need to have been paid during the period. It is simply an estimate (as accurate as possible) of the taxes that will need to be paid due to the income from this period.

Net Profit After Taxes = Profit Before Tax − Income Tax

The bottom-line profit that goes to the coffers of the company. Also known as NOPAT (Net Operating Profit After Taxes)

CASH FLOW STATEMENT

Both Balance Sheet and Income Statement are prepared based upon "Accrual Basis Accounting", according to which revenues are included when they are "earned" and costs are included when they are "incurred". It is not necessary for cash to have exchanged hands for revenue or expense to occur. Some people think that this leaves a lot of room for manipulation of Financial Statements by corporations, and rely on Cash Flow Statement. Cash

Flow Statement looks at Cash Flow through a period of time, and consists of three parts:
1) Cash Flow from Operations
2) Cash Flow from Investing activities
3) Cash Flow from Financing activities

Cash Flow from Operations (CFO) contains information about company's incoming and outgoing cash as a result of activity from its business operations. This includes most of the items in Income Statement like Sales, COGS, Operating Expenses, Tax etc. Taxes in CFO include only the actual tax paid. Also, since depreciation and amortization are non-cash charges, they are not included in the CFO.

Cash Flow from Investing includes activities like sale or purchase of assets (Property, Plant, Equipment, marketable securities etc.), loans made or received, Mergers & Acquisitions etc.

Cash Flow from Financing shows change in cash from activities related to company's investors, borrowers, and shareholders. It includes activities like proceeds and payment of debt, dividends, share buybacks, sale of company's stock etc.

Free Cash Flow (FCF): FCF is an important metric in Cash Flow Statement, and many investors consider it equivalent of Net Income from Income Statement. FCF can be described as the cash that is available to be distributed among various stakeholders of the company including Equity and Debt holders. FCF is the cash that the company generates from its business activities net of all costs needed to run the business. Most of these items are included in the Cash Flow from Operations. However, a company needs to keep making capital expenditures in order to keep running its operations, and as such are an integral part of company's business. So, FCF includes outflows due to Capital Expenditures also.

Free Cash Flow (FCF) = Cash Flow from Operations (CFO) − Capital Expense

Statement of Changes in Equity

Also known as Statement of Retained Earnings and Statement of Owner's Equity, this statement shows details of changes in owner's (or shareholders) equity and retained earnings over a period of time. For example, it shows how owner's equity or retained earnings changed as a result of operating income, dividends, sale or repurchase of stock etc. From investment analysis point of view, this statement is the least used among the four major financial statements.

FINANCIAL RATIOS

This section discusses important Financial Ratios and their calculation based upon various Financial Statements. These ratios can be grouped into various categories depending upon the main motive:

Profitability Ratios
These ratios measure how profitable a firm is compared to metrics like sales, equity, assets, investment etc.

Gross Margin: Calculates profit using only the direct product costs (Cost of Goods Sold) and excluding other operating expenses. It is considered as the most direct measure of profitability of company's products, as it does not include operating expenses which are largely fixed in nature.

$$Gross\ Margin = (Sales - Cost\ of\ Goods\ Sold) / Sales$$
$$= 1 - (COGS/Sales)$$

Operating Margin: This calculates profits based upon total costs, including operating expenses. This measures company's overall profitability (excluding taxes and interest).

Operating Margin = Operating Profit / Sales
= (Sales − COGS − Operating Expense) / Sales

Return on Assets (ROA): This measure calculates how profitable a company is relative to its assets. Please note that Assets are from Balance Sheet, and some parts like Land are calculated at the book value i.e. the price it was originally bought and may not reflect the true current market value of assets. Since Assets are measured at a single point of time, sometime average assets are used for this calculation (average of Assets at start and end of reporting period).

Return on Assets (ROA) = Net Income / Total Assets

Return on Equity (ROE): This is one of the more popular ratios, and measures the profitability of a company relative to the value of shareholder's equity. So it shows how much return the investors are getting for their investments.

Return on Equity (ROE) = Net Income / Shareholder's Equity

However, two things should be noted carefully. First, just like in ROA, *the value of Shareholder's Equity is derived from Balance Sheet, so it is the book value and may not accurately reflect the actual market value.* Real market value of company's equity is its Market Capitalization (Number of Shares * Share Price). Second, *this ratio can be distorted by debt.* For example, consider two companies with similar level of assets, but one takes on higher debt. Higher debt means lower Owners Equity. Now even if both earn exactly the same Income, ROE is higher for the company with higher debt. It doesn't necessarily mean that this company is being run more efficiently.

Return on Invested Capital (ROIC): It is pretty similar to ROE, however, instead of just owner's equity, it calculated profitability based upon invested capital of both equity and debt holders.

Return on Invested Capital (ROIC) = Net Income / (Long Term Debt + Shareholder's Equity)

Operating Efficiency Ratios

These ratios measure how efficiently a firm is utilizing its assets.

Asset Turnover: It calculates efficiency of a company in using its assets to generate revenues.

Asset Turnover = Sales / Total Assets

There are other similar ratios like Fixed Asset Turnover, that some people prefer to use under different circumstances.

Inventory Turnover: This ratio shows how many times a company's inventory is replaced over the reporting period. It is calculated as:

Inventory Turnover = Cost of Goods Sold (COGS) / Inventory

A higher Inventory Turnover is preferred as it means higher level of sales as well as lower inventory holding costs.

Days in Inventory: This measures the number of days per year that the company has to hold its inventory before selling.

Days in Inventory = 365 / Inventory Turnover

It is preferred to have lower number of Days in Inventory.

Leverage (Debt) Ratios

These ratios measure the relative level of a company's debt and its solvency.

Debt Ratio: It measures the total amount of a company's debt relative to its total assets.

Debt Ratio = Total Debt / Total Assets

This ratio helps provide a gauge about the level of leverage a company is using and whether or not it has sufficient resources to pay back its debt.

Some people use Total Debt to indicate Total Liabilities of a company (as noted in the Balance Sheet), while others prefer to use the term strictly to count only the short-term and long-term debt owed to debt-holders.

Debt-Equity Ratio: This ratio provides information about its capital structure in terms of ratio of invested capital from debt holders vs. equity holders

Debt-Equity Ratio = Total Debt / Owner's Equity

Liquidity Ratios
These ratios measure a firm's ability to be able to pay its short term obligations.

Current Ratio: It measures the total amount of a company's current liabilities relative to its current assets.

Current Ratio = Current Assets / Current Liabilities

This ratio includes all the current assets including Inventory.

Quick Ratio: It is more strict than Current ratio in that it excludes Inventory, as some of Inventory may not be easily liquidated.

$$Quick\ Ratio = (Current\ Assets - Inventory) / Current\ Liabilities$$

Cash Ratio: It is the most conservative ratio and uses only the cash and marketable securities in determining liquidity position.

$$Cash\ Ratio = (Cash + Marketable\ Securities) / Current\ Liabilities$$

MANAGERIAL ACCOUNTING

Introduction

Managerial Accounting is mostly concerned with the use of accounting information for strategic purposes and decision making by providing cost and profit information to the company management. Unlike Financial Accounting, this information is not intended to be reported outside the company, so it does not have to follow any accounting standards.

The main problem that it tries to solve is the classification of costs. For example, a company has several divisions and product segments. While it is easy to assign revenue breakdown among these, costs are more complicated as the same factory may be making different products, same workers may be working on projects belonging to different divisions or product lines, and then there are selling, marketing, and general administrative personnel that are supporting all the products. Once the costs are clearly broken down by segment, only then the management can learn about profitability levels for each segment and be able to make proper strategic decisions.

Topics in Brief

Costs: Classification of costs like Direct & Indirect costs, and Fixed / Variable costs.

Costing Methods: There are two main types of costing methods – 1) Traditional Costing (Standard Cost Accounting): Here overhead costs or indirect costs are allocated based upon the manufacturing volume metrics like units manufactured, direct labor time spent or machine time spent on production etc., and 2) Activity Based Costing (ABC): In this system, overhead costs are assigned to different products based upon each product's usage of that resource or activity.

Marginal Costing / Cost Volume Profit (CVP) Analysis: Marginal Costing and CVP Analysis show the relationship between revenues, costs and profits based upon fixed/variable costs and pricing. Based upon this analysis, a business owner or management can look at what minimum number of products they need to sell at a given price point to make profits or how to price the product to maximize profit. Also discusses concepts like Contribution Margin and Break-Even Volume.

Transfer Pricing: It discusses pricing mechanism when one part of the organization sells its products to another division of the same organization.

Costs

Direct vs. Indirect Costs: Direct Costs are the ones that can be completely attributed to a specific product, project or segment. Most important and common direct costs are Materials and Labor costs. Material costs are the expenses incurred on raw materials purchased for manufacturing a product, and Labor costs are the wages paid to workers.

Indirect costs are the overhead costs that cannot be allocated to a single product or segment and are mostly regarding shared resources. Some examples are Building costs, Supplies, Depreciation, Utilities, Selling & Administrative costs etc.

Fixed vs. Variable Costs: Another way to look at costs is whether the costs are fixed i.e. the company will have to incur those costs regardless of the production quantity, or if they are variable i.e. costs vary with the quantity produced. The classification of costs into fixed vs. variable categories becomes very important as the management tries to figure out how to best optimize the production quantity and whether it is feasible to start a product line or not. In practice, direct costs are mostly variable costs and indirect costs are mostly fixed costs, although there may be slightly different scenarios too.

Costing Methods
Using the costs discussed before as inputs, there are various methods of doing costing analysis that are used in decision making process.

Traditional Costing (Standard Cost Accounting): In Traditional Cost Accounting, overhead costs or indirect costs are allocated based upon the manufacturing volume metrics like units manufactured, direct labor time spent or machine time spent on production etc.

Advantages / Disadvantages: This method is relatively straight forward and simple to implement and also less costly. Also, it is aligned with Generally Accepted Accounting Principles (GAAP) standards. But the flip side is that it may not accurately capture the allocation of overhead costs and could result in wrong results. This is because this traditional method assumes that fixed costs are evenly spread over the volume, but in reality they may not be evenly spread. There could be a product that has high volume and take a large number of machine hours and direct labor hours for production, but is very simple to handle and doesn't require much technical and maintenance support. On the other hand, a specialized product with low production quantity and labor/machine hours could be highly complex and require a lot of maintenance. Under the traditional method, maintenance support costs would be distributed according to either the production volume or machine/labor hours, so a large part will be attributed to the simple product. But in reality, most of the maintenance support costs are related to the complex product. This could result in an erroneous analysis.

Activity Based Costing (ABC): In this system, overhead costs are assigned to different products based upon each product's usage of that resource or activity. First, total cost of an overhead activity is measured, then that cost is allocated among various products by determining the relative usage of that resource/activity by each product. Let's keep using the example discussed in Traditional Costing. If the total annual cost of maintenance department is $500,000 and the simple product (which is produced in large quantities) accounts for 20% of the maintenance usage, while the complex product (produced in smaller quantities) accounts for the rest 80%, then only 20% of the cost, which is $100,000, will be attributed to the simple product while the remaining $400,000 will be attributed to the complex product. Please note that in this system, it doesn't matter how much units of each products were produced or how much labor/machine hours they took.

Advantages / Disadvantages: This method provides the benefit of much more accurate information that can be used for decision making process. However, it is not easy to implement and requires lot of resources and costs. Also, it is not aligned with GAAP, so a company may need to have two sets of books – one for GAAP (Traditional Costing) and the other one for ABC.

Marginal Costing / Cost Volume Profit (CVP) Analysis
Marginal Costing and CVP Analysis show the relationship between revenues, costs, and profits based upon fixed/variable costs and pricing. As mentioned earlier, it is very important to accurately categorize fixed and variable costs as that can have a huge impact on the decision making. Based upon the CVP analysis, a business owner or management can look at what minimum number of products they need to sell at a given price point to make profits or how to price the product to maximize profit.

Contribution Margin: This tells about the profitability of a product based upon just the variable costs, and not taking into account the fixed costs at all. So if one assumes the fixed costs as given, then Contribution Margin tells about how much profit is made by selling every extra unit.

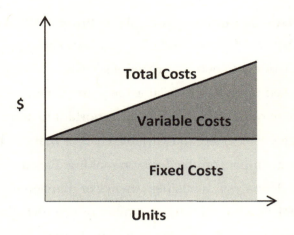

Total Costs = Fixed Costs + Variable Costs

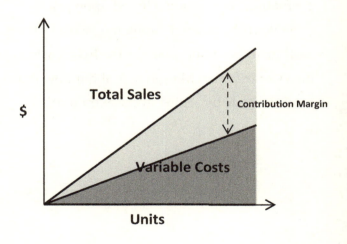

Contribution Margin = Total Sales − Variable Costs

Contribution Margin Ratio = Contrib. Margin / Sales
= (Sales − Variable Costs) / Sales
= 1 − Variable Costs / Sales

Here is how a company's profit statement looks with Contribution Margin and Fixed Costs:

Revenue
- Variable Costs

= Contribution Margin
 - Fixed Costs

 = Total Profit

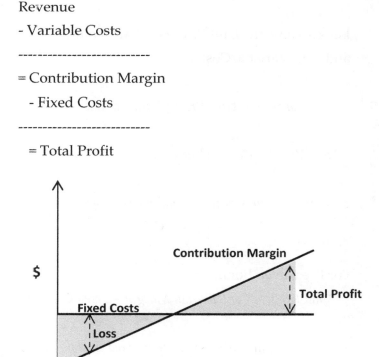

Total Profit (TP) = Contribution Margin − Fixed Costs

We can see that for a business to be profitable, the Contribution Margin should be higher than the Fixed Costs. This leads to next topic of discussion.

Break-Even Point Analysis: This analysis tells how many units a company should produce (at a given price point) to at least break even.

Let's assume the Unit Price is P, Unit Volume is V, and Unit Variable Cost is C

$$Total\ Sales = Unit\ Price * Unit\ Volume = P * V$$

$$Total\ Variable\ Cost = Unit\ Cost * Unit\ Volume = C * V$$

$$Contribution\ Margin = Total\ Sales - Variable\ Costs$$
$$= P * V - C * V$$

For Breakeven Point,
$$Total\ Profit = Contribution\ Margin - Fixed\ Costs = 0$$

$$Contribution\ Margin = Fixed\ Costs$$

$$P * V - C * V = Fixed\ Costs$$

$$V * (P - C) = Fixed\ Costs$$

$$V = Fixed\ Costs / (P - C)$$

Looking closely, (P – C) is nothing but Contribution Margin per unit (Sales Price – Variable Cost per Unit). So,

Break-even Volume = (Fixed Costs) / (Contrib. Margin per Unit)

A company can use these formulas to decide what combination of price and unit volume it must achieve to breakeven and maximize the profits.

Transfer Pricing

Another important topic in Managerial Accounting is Transfer Pricing. It is mostly of use in firms where there are multiple divisions with each having its own P&L (Profit & Loss) statements and where one division procures products from another one. Since it is within the same company, no exchange of cash takes place. But it is very important to account for this transfer of goods at appropriate value so that profitability of each division can be determined properly. There are few ways for accounting of Transfer Pricing:

Market Price: One way is to use market prices. If the divisions were not allowed to sell the products to each other, then one division would have to buy those from the external market and the other division could make money from selling the product in external market. So, using actual market price for that product can be considered as a fair value to be used in the Transfer Pricing. However, there are some issues with the use of Market Price. In case of some products, it may not be so easy to determine the market price. An example would be products sold to big corporations where pricing is highly negotiation based and varies from one customer to another. Another issue is that for selling within the company, the selling division doesn't need to incur any marketing or sales expense, so it should provide discount for that.

Negotiated Price: To deal with the issues related to Market Pricing, some companies prefer to use a Negotiated Price, where they let the Managers of the two divisions negotiate the price and come to an agreement. However, the cost of this strategy is time lost in negotiations, and resulting acrimony between executives within the company.

Profit based (Mark-up) Pricing: Another strategy is where the selling division is allowed to charge a certain fixed amount of profit for their products, and use the resulting price as the Transfer Price. The profit is usually based upon a "mark-up" price, i.e. a fixed percent above the cost. For example, a company allows 10% "mark-up" on costs. So, if a division produces product A at cost of $50 per unit, then its transfer price would be $50 +10% mark-up = $50 + $5 = $55.

OPERATIONS MANAGEMENT

Introduction
Operations Management has many definitions, but here we will define it as a discipline that deals with maximizing the efficiency and productivity within a company. While a big focus of this field has been related to manufacturing, most of the concepts can be applied to the Services and non-manufacturing aspects as well.

Topics in Brief

<u>Basic Operations Management Terms and Concepts:</u> Capacity, Throughput, Utilization, Cycle Time, Lead Time etc.

<u>Bottlenecks and Theory of Constraints:</u> Bottleneck usually means the resource that that takes the longest time in a process chain. According to the Theory of Constraints, the biggest bottleneck/constraint in the system dictates the overall throughput of the whole system. Managers should focus on identifying these bottlenecks and solving them.

Project Planning & Management Tools: These tools help figure out the most optimal way to achieve the project goals within the given resources and time. The two most common techniques are Critical Path Method (CPM) and Gantt Charts.

Supply Chain & Inventory Management: Discusses how to manage supply chain and inventories, and various concepts like Push-based Supply Chain, Bullwhip Effect (Whiplash Effect), Just-in-time (JIT) – Pull-based system, and Lean Manufacturing (Just-in-time JIT Production)

Basic Operations Management Terms and Concepts

There are few basic terms that one needs to learn to get better understanding of the subject.

Capacity: It is the maximum number of units that a machine can process in a given time. Capacity is expressed in terms of units per time, like 240 units per day or 10 units per hour.

Throughput: It is the actual number of units per time that are processed in a system in a given time. The main difference between Throughput and Capacity is that Throughput represents the actual number of units processed while Capacity is the maximum that can be processed. Throughput can also be calculated as inverse of Cycle Time (discussed below).

Utilization: It is ratio of how many units are processed vs. the real capacity. In other words, it is the ratio of Throughput to Capacity. It is usually represented in percentage.

Utilization = Throughput / Capacity

Cycle Time: It is the time between two successive units to come out of production or a process. For example, if an assembly line produces 30 units per hour, then the Cycle Time is 2 minutes per unit (60 minutes divided by 30 units). Cycle Time can also be thought of as equal to the inverse of Throughput.

Process Lead Time: It is the time to process one unit from beginning to end. For example, if a unit enters the production system at time 0 and emerges out of the processing system at time 10 minutes, then the Lead Time is 10 minutes.

(Please note that there is confusion between definition of Cycle Time and Lead Time in many publications, and our definition of Lead Time is sometimes referred to as Cycle Time)

WIP (Work-in-Process): This is the total number of units that are in the process at a time. In the above example, if a new unit enters the process system every 2 minutes, then there will be 5 units in the process at a given time. So WIP is 5 units.

Relationship between Lead Time, Throughput, and WIP: This relationship was first document by John Little, and is known as *Little's Law*. According to it, WIP in a system is Throughput times the Lead Time.

$$WIP = Throughput * Lead\ Time$$

EXAMPLE
To explain these terms, let's take example of a very simple system in which Raw Materials are processed by a Machine and converted into Finished Goods. In this example, empty cups and ingredient for ice creams are put in an Ice-cream Making Machine. This machine does everything from mixing the

ingredients to cooling/freezing, arranging the shape, and delivering a fully complete Ice-cream cup ready to eat. This machine has the Capacity to make 720 Ice-cream cups per hour, or 12 cups per minute. However, due to some other delays like labeling the cups, it takes 6 seconds to put the next cup in line. Also, it takes 30 seconds for an Ice-cream cup to be fully ready from the time it entered the machine. This whole process is summarized in the figure below.

Let us calculate various formulas from this process system:

Capacity = 12 cups per minute

Throughput = 1 / 6 seconds (*since time between two cups to enter the machine is 6 seconds*)
= 1 / 0.10 minutes = 10 *cups per minute*

Utilization = Throughput / Capacity
= 10/12 = 0.83 = 83%

Cycle Time = 6 seconds
(same as inverse of Throughput, 1/10 minutes = 6 seconds)

Lead Time = 30 seconds (time from beginning to end of the Ice-cream cup production)

WIP = Throughput * Lead Time
= 10 cups per minute * 0.5 minutes (30 seconds)
= 10 * 0.5 = 5 cups
(Note that the diagram also shows 5 cups in the machine at a time)

Bottlenecks and Theory of Constraints

Bottleneck usually means the resource that that takes the longest time in a process chain.

"Theory of Constraints" was created by Dr. Eliyahu Goldratt and first published in his popular 1984 book "The Goal". According to this theory, every system has one or more bottlenecks or constraints. The biggest bottleneck/constraint dictates the overall throughput of the whole system. Another way to think about it is that the chain is only as strong as its

weakest link. Managers should focus on identifying these bottlenecks and solving them.

Consider the Ice Cream Maker Machine example used before. Even though the Capacity of the machine is 12 cups per minute (or one cup every 5 seconds), the throughput is only 10 cups per minute (one cup every 6 seconds). So what's the bottleneck here? It is arranging or input of cups in the machine, which takes 6 seconds. Note that the total throughput is reduced to the throughput of the bottleneck.

One of the key takeaways here is that the overall Throughput cannot be higher than that of the bottleneck, and the only way to improve the throughput is by improving the bottleneck performance. One way to improve it is by maximizing the utilization of the bottleneck resource. Every possible thing should be done to make sure that the bottleneck resource is not allowed to sit idle. Every proper care should be taken so that it does not breakdown.
After identifying the bottleneck and trying to improve its efficiency (exploiting the bottleneck), the

next step is to subordinate everything else in the system to the bottleneck. It means that the focus of all the other processes should be on the bottleneck. The other processes should operate at same speed as the bottleneck, and if possible should try to take some load off the bottleneck resource. There is no point for other resources to work at higher throughput level than the bottleneck resource as that won't change the overall system throughput, which is always dictated by the bottleneck. It is better to provide some help to the bottleneck resource and improve its throughput.

The steps mentioned before are more of operational steps that managers can easily take after doing proper analysis and through proper resource allocation. If it still does not improve the bottleneck performance by the desired amount, then the next step is to "elevate the bottleneck" i.e. provide more resources and increase its capacity (either by putting more people or by buying new machine or upgrading it etc.), and often that would require extra investment. In that case, trade-offs need to be measured, but for any extra investment, bottleneck should be the biggest priority.

After undergoing these steps, go all over again to keep identifying the bottlenecks and improving their performance.

Project Planning & Management Tools
Any project can contain many different activities, resources with different capacities and speeds, interdependencies, time limits, goals etc. So it is very important to plan out these complex relationships and figure out the most optimal way to achieve the project goals within the given resources and time. Project Managers use various techniques to achieve this, and the two most common techniques are Critical Path Method (CPM) and Gantt Charts.

Critical Path Method (CPM): This methodology was initially developed by Morgan Walker and James Kelley in late 1950's. The CPM technique consists of making a diagram model of the project using three main inputs:
1) All the activities in the project
2) Time required to complete each activity
3) Dependencies between these activities

Just like Theory of Constraints focuses on identifying the bottleneck and improving it, CPM helps calculate the longest path (in terms of time) to complete the project. This path is called "Critical Path" and then the task for the management is to reduce this critical path. Let us take this example, where this *Activity Chart* shows various activities in a project, the time duration of each activity, and their dependencies:

Activity	Time Duration (hours)	Dependency
A	2	
B	5	A
C	4	A
D	6	A
E	3	B
F	6	B
G	5	C
H	3	D
I	6	E
J	4	F, G
K	3	G
L	5	H
M	1	I, J, K, L

Based upon this information, we can make a *CPM model* as shown below. The activities are shown as the nodes (little circles) in the diagram, with the time duration directly underneath, and dependency shown by arrows.

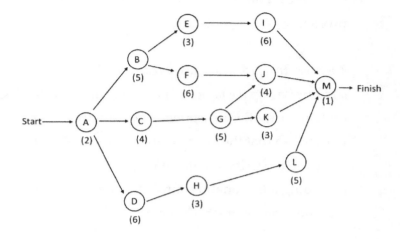

In this *CPM diagram*, there are 5 paths from Start to Finish:

ABEIM (2 + 5 + 3 + 6 + 1 = 17 hours)

ABFJM (2 + 5 + 6 + 4 + 1 = 18 hours)

ACGJM (2 + 4 + 5 + 3 + 1 = 15 hours)

ACGKM (2 + 4 + 5 + 3 + 1 = 14 hours)

ADHLM (2 + 6 + 3 + 5 + 1 = 17 hours)

The longest path is ABFJM, which takes 18 hours, and is the *Critical Path*. Any delay on any activity in the Critical Path will result in delays to the overall project.

There are two primary ways of reducing the Critical Path and speeding up the project: 1) Fast tracking – Instead of doing activities in sequence, some activities are retooled so that they can be done in parallel, thus reducing the Critical Path, and 2) Crashing – providing additional resources to some activities so that they can be finished sooner.

Gantt Chart: Named after its creator, Henry Gantt, these charts are very helpful in the scheduling of a project. Gantt chart has all the activities listed on the vertical axis and arranged such that the dependent activities are listed below the ones they are dependent upon. The horizontal axis represents the time (in hours, days, weeks, months etc.). For each activity, a horizontal bar is drawn, showing the time during which that activity will be completed. Thus, when one looks at a Gantt chart, it will look like flowing from top to bottom, and from left to right.

	Weeks						
	1	2	3	4	5	6	7
Task A	■						
Task B		■	■				
Task C		■	■	■			
Task D			■	■			
Task E				■	■		
Task F						■	■
Task G						■	■

Supply Chain & Inventory Management

One of the fundamental issues in Operations Management is managing supply chain and inventories.

A manufacturing company produces goods to sell to the consumers. First it needs to procure raw materials and other components from its suppliers. Then it uses those in its production facilities to manufacture finished goods. These finished goods are then sent off to retailers (like Wal-Mart, Target, Best-Buy etc.) through distributors or wholesalers. The retail stores finally sell the goods to the consumers.

Here is an overview of how overall supply chain works, and shows the typical flow from raw materials to finished goods in customer's hands.

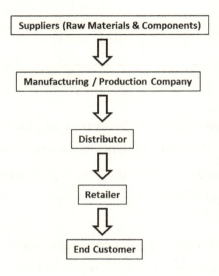

It is very important to understand that nobody in the supply chain knows for sure how many items the consumers are going to purchase. There are two main strategies that companies can use to manage their distribution/inventory – Push and Pull based.

Push-based Supply Chain: Here every company at different steps in supply chain makes its production plans based upon its own internal forecast about orders from its immediate customer. Normally this forecasting is done based upon the historical order patterns, with same adjustments to take into account overall current economic situation. So it is also called *Forecasting based supply chain management*. Since nobody wants to be in a situation where they run out of goods while customer demand is still there, Retailers want some extra units on hand just in case. This is called "Inventory". Similarly, Distributors want some inventory for Retailers, and this goes on until the very end of this chain – Suppliers. Thus, Inventory is built up at every step in this Supply Chain. But inventory always costs money – in terms of space and also money tied up in buying it before it can be sold. So every company tries its best to minimize inventory, while at the same time making sure that sales are not impacted due to not having enough products on hand.

Bullwhip Effect (Whiplash Effect): This is a trend seen in push based systems, where the swings in inventory become bigger and bigger as one moves back in the supply chain. It normally happens when there is sudden change in consumer demand. The biggest reasons for this effect are the need for inventory buffers, which are necessary due to forecast errors (as a company can rarely forecast the future demand accurately). These buffers, and the resulting swings, get bigger from retailer to suppliers at the other end of the supply chain. An underlying cause is very little visibility into the end consumer demand for the downstream suppliers, with their only source of knowledge being their own immediate customers.

<u>Just-in-time (JIT) – Pull-based system:</u> To deal with disadvantages of push-based supply chain, some companies use pull-based system, also known as by its more famous term, Just-in-time (JIT) system. Here the entire system works backwards, and the whole process is demand driven instead of forecast driven. Instead of the process getting started with raw material supplies, it starts with consumer demand. As the consumer buy products from the retailer, the retailer orders more products from the distributor, which in turn orders more from the manufacturer, and the chain goes all the way back to the raw material suppliers. As one can see, this way there is no additional inventory in the entire supply chain. However, this system runs into problem when there

is sudden excess demand for a product.
Manufacturer or suppliers may not be able to meet with this sudden rush and end up losing revenues due to that. Also, this system depends a lot on timely and accurate data flow throughout the supply chain. Speed is very important in JIT systems.

Lean Manufacturing (Just-in-time JIT Production):
This concept is used in production and is very similar to pull-based inventory management. This was first developed in Japan by Toyota, and implemented in their factories. So, it is also called Toyota Production System (TPS), and later evolved into "Lean Manufacturing". What better way to learn more about it than hearing from the original developer itself.
Here is how this process is described on Toyota's website:

Just-in-Time (Productivity improvement)
- Making only "what is needed, when it is needed, and in the amount needed!"
Producing quality products efficiently through the complete elimination of waste, inconsistencies, and unreasonable requirements on the production line.

In order to deliver a vehicle ordered by a customer as quickly as possible, the vehicle is efficiently built within the shortest possible period of time by adhering to the following:

1. *When a vehicle order is received, a production instruction must be issued to the beginning of the vehicle production line as soon as possible.*
2. *The assembly line must be stocked with required number of all needed parts so that any type of ordered vehicle can be assembled.*
3. *The assembly line must replace the parts used by retrieving the same number of parts from the parts-producing process (the preceding process).*
4. *The preceding process must be stocked with small numbers of all types of parts and produce only the numbers of parts that were retrieved by an operator from the next process.*

Source:
http://www.toyota-global.com/company/vision_philosophy/toyota_production_system/

FINANCE

Introduction – It's all about Capital Allocation

Finance is a broad discipline, but at its very heart the main theme is to use capital (or cash) and grow it with maximum efficiency. In effect, it deals with the most optimal allocation of capital in various investments to generate the best possible return. Take any Finance sub-discipline, be it capital projects, equity investments, bonds, foreign exchange, derivatives, real estate etc., it is all about growing/preserving capital at various risk levels. Unlike other fields like Marketing, Operations or Strategy, value is not created by doing or creating something new or increasing productivity or selling something. In Finance, the source of value creation is efficient capital allocation. There are many different ways and strategies to do it, but the bottom line is capital allocation.

Topics in Brief

Risk and Return: Investors seek Return with their investments which entail some Risk. This statement can also be flipped to say that people take on risky investments and seek appropriate reward as returns.

Riskier the investment, higher the expectation of returns.

Time Value of Money: Value of a dollar today is not the same as what it was one year ago or what it will be one year from now. The value of money changes with time. Why? Because of expectations of "return". Future Value after n years, at discount rate r can be represented as: $FV = PV * (1 + r)^n$

Net Present Value (NPV) and Internal Rate of Return (IRR): NPV is total sum of present values of cash inflows and outflows over time, after adjusting for the discount rates. IRR is in effect the discount rate at which NPV of a project becomes zero. IRR tries to calculate the return rate for a given project.

Capital Structure and Cost of Capital: A company's capital consists of two main sources – debt and equity. Equity owners have stake in the firm and get paid through the profits earned by the company. Company's debt holders have no ownership stake in the company and don't share profits, and get paid through interest payments on their loans, and full repayment of loans. A company's total cost of capital is weighted average of its cost of equity and its cost of debt. It is weighted based upon company's capital structure (debt/equity mix).

Capital Asset Pricing Model (CAPM) and Securilty Market Line (SML): This is a model used to determine the expected rate of return for a security (stock). The formula is:

Expected Return = Risk-free Rate + Beta * Market Risk Premium

SML can be described as a graphical representation of CAPM.

Risks, Diversification, and Portfolio Performance Measurement: For Portfolio Management, Risk is measured by Standard Deviation of Returns. Higher the standard deviation, higher the Beta and Risk. There are two types of risks – Specific Risk and Systematic Risk.

Equity Valuation: Techniques to value Equities
- Discounted Cash Flow (DCF) Analysis
- Dividend Discount Model (DDM) Analysis

<u>Relative or Comparative Valuation Approaches:</u>
Another popular set of valuation technique, where a company's Price is compared to others in the same industry or with similar characteristics:
- Price to Earnings Ratio (P/E)
- Earnings Yield
- Price to Sales Ratio (P/S)
- Price to Book Value Ratio (P/B)

Risk, Return, and Opportunity Cost
Another very basic concept in Finance is the relationship between risk and return (or reward), and also the opportunity cost. It is fundamental to almost everything in this field. (Here the assumption is that the investments that we are discussing are made with expectation of growth in capital (in other words - Return) and are not done for other purposes like recreation, lifestyle, charity etc. Any investment of capital entails risk. It could range from investing in new farming equipment to buying stocks to keeping money in bank savings account. <u>But what is Risk? In simple words, Risk is the probability of investments not generating the desired returns or of losing money (negative returns)</u>.

In other words, investors seek Return with their investments which entail some Risk. This statement can also be flipped to say that people take on risky investments and seek appropriate reward as returns. Riskier the investment, higher the expectation of returns.

There is one thing that should be very clear in mind – riskier investment does not entitle anybody to higher return. An investor seeks higher returns to compensate for the higher risk. And by definition, risk is that those expected returns never come through. So, always keep in mind that risk is real and could actually happen.

Opportunity Cost also has a role to play in this. Since capital is a limited resource, the opportunity cost is use of this capital in other investments. So investors look around for investment that provides the best return for a given amount of risk, or the investment with a given amount of reward but with the least risk. This has large implications in Portfolio Theory and Management as we will see later.

Discount Rate (Rate of Return)

One term that will keep appearing throughout this chapter is Discount Rate or rate of Return. In simple terms, this is the return that investors expect when they invest in a business or project. Different projects or investments will have different discount rates, depending upon their riskiness. The investors estimate the discount rate for a new investment based upon the rate of return they will get from other existing investments with a similar risk profile. This rate of return is also used for discounting future cash flows, as we will see in next few topics, and is different for different investments.

Time Value of Money

After Risk and Return, Time Value of Money is another fundamental topic in Finance, and crucial in understanding of various valuation techniques. The basic rule to keep in mind is that value of a dollar today is not the same as what it was one year ago or what it will be one year from now. The value of money changes with time. Why? Answer is because of expectations of "return". A good example would be interest earned on money. Let's say a person has $100 today. He deposits that money in a savings account which provides 15% interest rate. In one year, the money will grow to $115. So, value of $115 in one year is equivalent to that of $100 now. If PV denotes Present Value of money, FV the Future Value, and *r* is the Rate (Interest Rate, also known as Discount rate), then

$$FV = PV * (1 + r)$$

If we want to calculate the value after five years, it will be as follows:

*After 1 year: 100 * (1 + 15%) = 100 * 1.15 = $115*
*After 2 years: 105 * (1 + 15%) = 105 * 1.15 = $132.25*
*After 3 years: 110.25 * (1 + 15%) = 110.25 * 1.15 = $152.09*
*After 4 years: 115.76 * (1 + 15%) = 115.76 * 1.15 = $174.90*
*After 5 years: 121.55 * (1 + 15%) = 121.55 * 1.15 = $201.14*

It seems cumbersome to do these 5 steps, but it you look carefully, all the steps above can be consolidated into one single step:
$100 * 1.15 * 1.15 * 1.15 * 1.15 * 1.15 = $100 * (1 + .05)^{5}

Thus, Future Value after n years, at discount rate r can be represented as:

$$FV = PV * (1 + r)^n$$

This is also known as Compounding Effect.
This is a very powerful concept that is used at many places in our daily lives.

Take a look again at the example above. *After five years, the money has grown to $201, slightly <u>more than double</u> the original amount*, based upon 15% interest per year.

<u>How did it happen?</u> The key is to realize that the interest gained every year is also being re-invested and creates additional gains. This keeps becoming bigger every year.

Here are some other eye-popping facts from the miracle of compounding:
<u>If one starts with $1 and keeps doubling that money every year, after ten years it would become $1,024. Yes, more than 1000 times the original amount in 10 years.</u> Here is the chart that explains the growth:

Year	0	1	2	3	4	5	6	7	8	9	10
Amount	$1	$2	$4	$8	$16	$32	$64	$128	$256	$512	$1,024

You have already seen the example where 15% rate leads to doubling of money in 5 years.
Do you know, what <u>20% growth rate</u> will do? It will almost <u>Triple</u> the money in six years.
What about <u>25% growth rate</u> of money?
A: Tripling of money in five years.

Let's use our formula to make sure:
20% growth per year, total 6 years: $FV = \$100 * (1 + .20)^6 = \$299$
25% growth per year, total 5 years: $FV = \$100 * (1 + .25)^5 = \$305$

Let's look at it the other way around. *If someone says he/she can double your money in 5 years or triple your money in 6 years, you should be able to calculate backwards, and know that he/she is talking about 15% or 20% returns per year.* Although these are pretty good returns, but they sound extremely impressive when expressed in terms of doubling or tripling of money. Here is a quick cheat-sheet to show relationship between rate of return (per year) and time to double/triple initial investment:

Annual Rate of Return	Time to Double	Time to Triple
15%	5 years	8 years
20%	4 years	6 years
25%	3 years	5 years

This formula can be applied in reverse too. If the value of Future cash flow is known, then we can use the discount rate to find the Present Value of those future cash flows.

$$PV = FV \div (1 + r)^n$$

What does it mean? Take our previous example of 15% return. Here it means that if the discount rate (or expected rate of return) is 15%, then if you get $115 one year from now, its Present Value right now is $100. Why? Because if you have $100 now and invested in a similar project with 15% return, you would still receive $115 one year from now. Take another example: Somebody promises to pay you $200 in five years if you invest $100 now. To see if $200 five years from now is worth $100 now, you can check the Present Value of $200 five years out. However, you need to be first given a proper discount rate. You thoroughly check the market and find out that other investments with a similar risk profile are paying 25% returns per year. Now that you have the discount rate, you can calculate the PV of that future amount of money. We plug in the values in our formula:

$$PV = 200 \div (1 + 0.25)^5 = 200 \div (1.25)^5 = 200 \div 3.05$$
$$= \$65.54$$

So, PV of $200 future payment in five years is only $65.54 given a discount rate of 25%. Paying $100 now would be too much, and is not a good investment.

Present Value of a Perpetuity: Annuity refers to a stream of fixed payments over a specified period of time. Perpetuity is a special kind of Annuity where there is no end or time limit, and the fixed payments continue forever. While PV for annuities can be calculated by finding PV of each annuity and then adding them up, it is hard to do for a forever continuing perpetuity. Thankfully, there is a simple mathematical formula for calculating PV of a Perpetuity. If the value of fixed payment cash stream (per year) is C, and annual discount rate is r, then its PV is:

$$PV = C / r$$

For example, PV of a perpetual annuity stream of $100 per year at a discount rate of 5% is:

$$PV = 100 / 5\% = 100 / 0.05 = \$2,000$$

Present Value of a Perpetuity with Growth: If the perpetuity keeps growing every year at a growth rate of g, and C is the first installment at end of the first year, then PV is calculated as:

$$PV = C / (r - g)$$

Net Present Value (NPV)

NPV is total sum of present values of cash inflows and outflows over time (including current and future). In the example discussed before, PV of future cash inflows was $65.54, and current cash outflow was $100. So,

$$NPV = -100 + 65.54 = -34.46$$

To calculate NPV, first the PV of each cash outflow or inflow is calculated (using the discount rate), and then all the PVs are added up. If there is a cash flow at the current time, then it is already equal to its Present Value.

Use of NPV: NPV is mostly used to calculate if a project is worthy of investment, especially at a company level. If the NPV is greater than zero, it means that the project will add value to the company and should go ahead. If it is less than zero, then the investment should not be made. If NPV is 0, then this project neither adds value nor loses any money.

NPV is also used to compare the profitability of two projects when a decision needs to be made to choose only one project. The project with the highest NPV is the one that should be selected. But, couple of things need to be kept in mind when comparing the projects: 1) The discount rate can change the results i.e. for one discount rate Project A may have higher NPV but if the discount rate is changed to another value then Project B may have higher NPV, 2) Since

NPV only shows the absolute value of money, it tends to favor projects with higher initial investment. For example a project with initial investment of $100 has $80 in NPV (which is pretty good return), but another project with initial investment of $250 has $90 NPV. NPV analysis will suggest adoption of project B as it has higher NPV, but intuitively we know that return on investment is not as good as it is in Project A. So, it is better to use NPV analysis for projects with similar investments.

Internal Rate of Return (IRR)

IRR tries to calculate the return rate for a given project. A project is considered good and worth accepting if the IRR is higher than a pre-determined minimum rate of return. Usually this minimum acceptable rate is company's cost of capital.

IRR is calculated as the discount rate at which NPV of a project becomes zero. So, if one knows the cash inflows and outflows, then calculate the discount rate for which NPV is 0.

The main purpose of IRR is for decision making in selection of projects based upon the highest rate of return. This is different than NPV which selects based upon the highest amount of dollars in NPV. IRR helps deal with the problem of using NPV in projects with different investments, but it has its own set of issues.

<u>Issues with IRR:</u> For a project to be accepted, IRR should be higher than the discount rate. However, if the discount rate is unclear or changes over time, then it becomes difficult to use IRR for accepting or rejecting a project. Second, there are cases when there are both cash inflows and outflows in future (vs. a simple case of outflow in the beginning and then a series of inflows). In such case, there can be two or more IRRs that can make NPV zero. So, it becomes hard to know which IRR to use for the decision.

Evidence suggests that company executives prefer IRR over NPV as it is easier to compare two projects of different sizes, which is the most common situation.

Pay-back Period

This is an old concept and simply calculates the time required for the project to pay back its initial investment. It does not use time value of money. For example, a project costs $100 in the beginning and pays back $25 every year. The project's pay-back period will be simply when it returns the initial $100, which will be 4 years. Projects with shorter pay back periods are preferred over the ones with longer periods. This concept has serious limitations as it does not take into account discount rate or time value of money, but is very simple and intuitive to use.

Capital Structure – Debt & Equity

A company's capital consists of two main sources – debt and equity. In other words, a company is financed by either equity (owner's capital) or debt (borrowings or loans from other sources). Equity owners have stake in the firm and get paid through the profits earned by the company. Company's debt holders have no ownership stake in the company and don't share profits, and get paid through interest payments on their loans, and full repayment of loans.

Debt Interest Rates and Credit ratings: Interest on Debt or Loans depends upon the credit worthiness of the borrowing company. A company in sound shape is considered less risky and thus gets loans at lower interest rates. As the riskiness of the company increases, the interest rates get higher. There are credit rating agencies like S&P, Moody's, Fitch etc. which rate a company's credit worthiness. The best rating (by S&P and Fitch) is AAA and worst is C. Anything below C means a company is already in default, meaning it has failed to pay its debt obligations (interest payments or loan repayments).

Need for Debt: As mentioned earlier, there are two main sources of raising capital (capital is required either to start up a new company, or for financing of company expansion, upgrade of machinery, newer investments, etc.) – 1) Owners put their own money or get new partners, 2) Owners borrow money from banks or other lending institutions.

The problems with the first option start occurring when the company needs additional capital for expansion or other investment projects. At that time either the existing owners don't have enough cash or are unwilling to put more of their money (for a variety of reasons). Then they are faced with two choices – expansion of owner's equity by seeking new partners, or getting loan. The main issue with new partners (or shareholders) is that it dilutes the ownership stake of existing partners. For example, a company owned by ten equal partners is worth $1 million and needs to raise additional $500,000. If they get new partners, ownership stake of each existing partner will go down from 10% to 6.7%. On the other hand, if they borrow money from a lending institution, their stake will remain 10%, although they will have to pay interest on that loan.

This leads to one of the biggest financial issues faced by companies – <u>what is the optimal capital structure?</u> i.e. How much of the company should be financed by debt and how much by equity? There is another issue that comes into play that we will discuss now – cost of debt and cost of equity.
On balance, cost of debt is lower but risk of default and need to pay interest. More equity means dilution of existing shareholder equity.

Cost of Capital

A company's total cost of capital consists of two parts – cost of debt and cost of equity. The weighted average of these two is called Weighted Average Cost of Capital (WACC), which is the company's total cost of capital. So, f a company's capital V consists of Equity E and Debt D, and its cost of debt is R_d and cost of equity is R_e then its WACC is:

$$WACC = R_e * (E/V) + R_d * (D/V)$$

<u>Cost of Debt:</u> This is relatively straightforward to measure by the interest rate charged on the loans received by the company. If a company has multiple loans at different rates, then a weighted average is sued to measure the total cost of debt. Average cost of debt for US public companies is around 3-4%.
Source:
http://people.stern.nyu.edu/adamodar/New_Home_Page/datafile/wacc.htm

Another thing to keep in mind is that in most cases, debt interest expense is tax deductible. So actual cost of debt is lower, depending upon the company's tax rate, and this lower number is used in the actual calculation of WACC.

Cost of Equity: This is the return that investors expect when they invest in a company's equity by buying its shares. Another way to think about it from an existing owner's perspective is that if they have some amount of capital that they can invest in this company, what are the returns they can expect if this investment is made (by buying shares) in another company with similar risk profile? That return rate is their cost of equity. So, cost of equity is determined by the returns expected by overall market for that company. There is a formula to derive a company's cost of equity and uses the CAPM, which we discuss next. Average Cost of Equity in US is around 9 – 10%.

Capital Asset Pricing Model (CAPM)

This is a model used to determine the expected rate of return for a security (stock). The formula is:

$$E = R_f + \beta \, (R_m - R_f)$$

where,

E	= Expected Rate of Return
R_f	= Risk Free Rate
R_m	= Rate of Return for the Market
$R_m - R_f$	= Market Risk Premium
β	= Beta (Security's sensitivity to market risk)

*Expected Return = Risk-free rate + Beta * Market Risk Premium*

R_f *(Risk Free Rate)* - This is the rate of return on investments that theoretically have zero risk. US Treasury Bills/Bonds are considered to have zero default risk, and generally 10 year Treasury Bond Yield is used as a proxy for Risk-free rate. Its value is currently around 2-3%.

R_m *(Market Rate of Return)* - This represents the rate of return for the entire market (This differentiation between market return and individual stock return is very important in Portfolio Management). Usually the average of historical returns (S&P 500) is used to calculate this market return rate. It is generally accepted that historical long-term average return for US market is around 9-10%.

Market Risk Premium - This is the difference between market return rate and risk-free rate. This tells about how much extra (premium) returns investors expect to receive (vs. risk free rate) by investing in a given market. This number is different across various countries. It is estimated that current market risk premium in US is around 6%. Different scholars have different interpretations and calculations for Market Risk Premium, and historical estimates (for US market) range from around 4 – 6%.

β *(Beta)* - It measures the sensitivity of a stock to the whole market by calculating the correlation between volatility in the stock to the volatility of the market. In other words, it measures the relationship between change in the stock price to change in the overall market. When the relative change in both is same, this ratio is 1, so Beta = 1. If stock changes more than the market, then $\beta > 1$, when the change is in the same direction but lower than the market then Beta is between 0 and 1, and when the change is in opposite direction i.e. stock gains while market loses or vice-versa, $\beta < 0$. By looking at the CAPM formula, one can easily see that the only stock specific factor in determining the Expected rate of return is Beta. Everything else is dependent upon overall market data (Risk-free Rate and Market Risk Premium). Stocks with higher Beta are considered more risky and hence investors expect or demand higher rate of return.

Security Market Line (SML)

SML is a graphical representation of CAPM. The graph shows relationship between Expected Returns on y-axis and Beta of a security on the x-axis. The line intercepts the y-axis at Risk-free rate (where Beta is zero). Market Risk Premium $(R_m - R_f)$ is represented by slope of the line.

After plotting the SML, different securities are placed on this graph based upon their exposure to market risk (Beta) and Expected Returns. Any given point on the SML shows expected return for a security with the corresponding Beta. Securities that are above the SML are considered good investments, while those below are not.

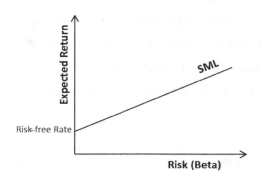

Movement of SML: SML can move in two ways – 1) It can shift up or down, and 2) Its slope can change.

Parallel movement (up or down) usually occurs due to change in inflation expectations. Slope of the line stays same, but with higher inflation expectations, expected return is higher for a given Beta. Risk-free rate also moves up.

Slope of the line, which represents Market Risk Premium, changes based upon risk-reward profile or when investors become more risk-averse or ready to take more risk. This could happen due to change in market conditions and state of the economy.

Risk and Diversification

For Portfolio Management, Risk is measured by Standard Deviation of Returns. Higher the standard deviation, higher the Beta and the Risk. There are two types of risks – Specific Risk and Systematic Risk.

Specific Risk, as the name implies, is specific to an individual security or a small group of securities. Examples include some natural disaster in a small region, new regulation affecting a single or just a few companies, customer demand shift, a company losing market share etc. Although every company has some sort of Specific Risk, this risk can be diversified away by holding a diversified portfolio of securities. Remember that there is also positive Specific Risk associated with each asset, and that too is diversified away. The underlying belief is that in a well-diversified portfolio, a negative specific risk associated event in one security will be matched by a positive event in another asset. This is why Specific Risk is also known as *Diversifiable Risk*.

Systematic Risk, also known as Market Risk and Un-diversifiable Risk, represents the risk relating to the entire market. Examples include a country falling into recession, national calamity, tax increase etc. This risk affects the entire market and cannot be diversified away.

This is why investors seek to hold diversified portfolio of stocks, so that they can diversify away the Specific Risk of individual stocks, and only remaining risk is the Systematic Risk.

Portfolio Performance Measurement

Since most of the investments are managed as a Portfolio, it is important to be able to objectively measure and evaluate the performance of a Portfolio so that different Investment Managers can be evaluated and compared. There are three main measures to do this:

Treynor Measure: This is based upon the concept of SML (whose creator was Jack Treynor), and measures excess portfolio return (vs. risk-free rate) in relation to Beta of the portfolio.

Treynor Measure T = (Portfolio Return − Risk-free Rate) / Portfolio's Beta

Sharpe Ratio: This is almost identical to the Treynor Measure, except that the risk is measured by Standard Deviation of the portfolio instead of its Beta.

Sharpe ratio S = (Portfolio Return − Risk-free Rate) / Portfolio's Std. Dev.

<u>Jensen's Alpha:</u> This is different than the other two measures in that it calculates the excess return of a portfolio compared to its expected benchmark return based on CAPM. Looking at the SML graph, it measures the difference between actual return on the graph vs. expected return on SML for same Beta.

Jensen's Alpha α = Actual Portfolio Return – Benchmark Portfolio Return

Jensen's Alpha measures a portfolio manager's ability to generate excess returns (alpha) based upon his/her own ability rather than just taking on risky investments.

Equity Valuation

This is one of the more popular topics in Finance. How to Value a company? There are hundreds of books and articles written on this topic, and thousands of stock investors seek answer to this question daily. Frankly, there is no single right answer for this, if there were, we wouldn't see stock market fluctuations. It is said that Valuation is more art than science, and truly so. What we can discuss here is the techniques that are taught in the MBA programs and used by finance professionals.

NOTE: While some of these methods will appear easy, they are hardly so. While the calculations part is straightforward, hard part is assumptions you put in place to estimate items like future revenue growth, gross margins, operating expenses etc. The actual outcomes are nearly impossible to predict. While doing any valuation analysis, please remember one golden rule: **The whole valuation analysis is only as good as the assumptions that go in.** Otherwise it is of no value.

Discounted Cash Flow (DCF):
DCF analysis stems directly from Time Value of Money concept discussed in the very beginning of this chapter. The underlying concept is that you estimate Cash Flow for each period (usually a year) that goes to the investors – Free Cash Flow (discussed in Financial Accounting) is a popular measure for this estimate, determine appropriate Cost of Capital for the company, and discount these Future Cash Flows to their Present Value. Then you

add existing Cash and subtract any debt to arrive at company's true value.

If r is the cost of capital for the company (WACC, in case company has debt), and CF_n denote cash flow for the nth period, then PV of these cash flows can be calculated as:

$$PV = \frac{CF_1}{(1+r)} + \frac{CF_2}{(1+r)^2} + \frac{CF_3}{(1+r)^3} + \frac{CF_4}{(1+r)^4} + \frac{CF_5}{(1+r)^5} + \cdots$$

Since future cash flows are based on many assumptions and estimates, it becomes very hard to predict those after a few years. The normal method for calculating value beyond a certain amount of years is using Terminal Value. Here after certain amount of years, a fixed perpetual growth rate is assumed for the cash flows. In the above example, let's say that after five years, Cash flows will keep growing in perpetuity at a growth rate of g. Then according to the Gordon Growth Model, Terminal Value can be calculated as:

$$TV = \frac{CF_6}{(r-g)}$$

As we are assuming growth rate of g after 5th year,
$CF_6 = CF_5 * (1 + g)$

So, Terminal Value can be re-written as:

$$TV = \frac{CF_5 \times (1 + g)}{(r - g)}$$

Now, Present Value of the future cash flows can be written as:

$$PV = \frac{CF_1}{(1+r)} + \frac{CF_2}{(1+r)^2} + \frac{CF_3}{(1+r)^3} + \frac{CF_4}{(1+r)^4} + \frac{CF_5}{(1+r)^5} + \text{Terminal Value}$$

To calculate Total Company Fair Value for Equity holders, we subtract company's net debt (Total Debt less existing Cash) from this Present Value of future cash flows.

Fair Value$_{Equity}$ = PV – Net Debt = PV + Existing Cash – Total Debt

There is one more thing we need to figure out in detail – how to estimate the cash flows. Here is a chart to derive Free Cash Flow for a company:

Revenue
- Cost of Goods Sold
= *Gross Profit*
  - Operating Expenses
  = *Operating Profit*
    - Taxes
    = *Net Operating Profit after Tax (NOPAT)*
      - Capital Expenditure
      - Net Working Capital changes
      = *Free Cash Flow (FCF)*

FCF = Revenue − COGS − Operating Expenses − Taxes − Capital Expenditures − WC changes

FCF = NOPAT − Capital Expenditures − Net Working Capital Changes

For the DCF analysis, one usually starts from the current year financials. Then Y/Y (year over year) Revenue growth is estimated for next few years. Then COGS and Operating expenses are estimated as percentage of sales for the future, along with estimated tax rates. This will give NOPAT estimate for the future. Then the Capital expenditures (again as percentage of revenues) are estimated, and then changes to Net Working Capital (this normally is brought down to zero over time). This provides estimated Free Cash Flow (to both equity and debt holders) for the coming years. As discussed earlier, since it is not possible to forecast many years out in the future without huge errors, Terminal Value of FCF is calculated after few years of projections.

Once we have all these projections, these cash flows are discounted over time using company's Cost of Capital or WACC to calculate the Present Value. This gives the Present Value of the company's cash flows to Company's capital holders, which include both the equity as well as the debt holders. To calculate company's equity value, we simply subtract company's Net Debt from the PV of cash flows.

Dividend Discount Model (DDM)
In many ways this model is similar to DCF, but there is one big difference. Instead of Free Cash Flow, it uses Dividends. Since Dividends go directly to the shareholders, this model calculates the Equity value of the company. The main assumption in DDM is that Dividends are the only real cash flow that equity investors (share-holders) are going to get, since the

company is assumed to be an on-going entity. Based upon this assumption, Present Value of future dividends is the Intrinsic Value of the company.

The simplicity as well as the biggest problem of the model lies within this assumption. It is a very easy model to use, and to some extent the thinking is valid that only real cash flow that the investors will see is dividends. But it does not take into account the fact that the Dividend is not the only way for the companies to return cash to the share-holders. Some companies use share buybacks instead of dividends. Another issue is that some companies prefer to keep lots of cash for future investments or M&A activities. Also, even in the case of dividend issuing companies, dividends may not be stable and can fluctuate over time, with zero dividends at some time. There also have been cases of some companies giving out huge one time dividends. These issues make it hard to estimate Dividends and value companies on this basis. Anyway, here is the theoretical calculation to measure the Price of a company at time 0 based upon expected dividends D, and Cost of Equity r (note that it is just Equity

Cost and not WACC or Cost of Capital since this is only for Equity holders).

$$P_0 = \frac{D_1}{(1+r)} + \frac{D_2}{(1+r)^2} + \frac{D_3}{(1+r)^3} + \frac{D_4}{(1+r)^4} + \frac{D_5}{(1+r)^5} + \text{Terminal Value}$$

In cases where there is no expectation of any growth in dividends,

$$P_0 = \frac{D_1}{r}$$

In cases where Dividends are expected to grow perpetually at growth rate of *g*, the following calculation is used. This is also known as Gordon Growth model, after its creator Myron Gordon.

$$P_0 = \frac{D_1}{(r-g)}$$

Relative or Comparative Valuation Approaches
There is another popular set of valuation technique, and here a company's Price is compared to others in the same industry or with similar characteristics, based upon different metrics like Earnings, Sales, Book Value etc.

Price to Earnings Ratio (P/E): This is perhaps the most popular relative valuation measure. It is the ratio of the current stock price to its EPS (Earnings Per Share). EPS can be for the current fiscal year or an estimate of the next fiscal year. Sometimes Next Twelve Months (NTM) or Last/Trailing Twelve Months (LTM) are also used.

When valuing a company, a peer set of companies (normally within the same industry) is used to measure their P/E ratios. It is very subjective choice, depending upon each individual, about which companies to use in the peer set. Some may chose only very few (even only one) companies that are very similar to the company being valued, while others may use a much broader set. Here are the steps to value a company's stock price based upon P/E relative valuation:
- Prices are already known for other companies, and for Earnings or EPS estimates, normally an average of Analyst Estimates (Wall Street Equity Analysts) is used.
- Second step is to calculate the average P/E for these companies.

- Then an estimate of EPS for current or next fiscal year is forecasted using assumptions for Revenue Growth, Profit Margins etc.
- Finally, the average peer P/E ratio is multiplied by the EPS estimate to calculate the stock's Price. Again, please note that this is just an estimate with the fundamental assumption that this company should have same P/E as its peer companies.

What does P/E tell us? First, let's revisit the Gordon Growth Model to value a company with constant growth rate. Let us use Earnings (E) instead of Dividends, with the assumption that Earnings of a company are the true measure of its cash/income generation. With growth rate of g and cost of equity r, its Price is:

$$P_0 = \frac{E_1}{(r-g)} = \frac{E_0(1+g)}{(r-g)}$$

So, if Price and Current Earnings are known, then ratio of Price to Earnings becomes:

$$\frac{P_0}{E_0} = \frac{(1+g)}{(r-g)}$$

So the P/E ratio gives us some information about market's expectations of future growth of the company (growth rate, g) as well as its riskiness (discount rate, r). This is why companies with high growth expectations have higher P/E ratios, and risky companies have lower P/E ratio. In other words, if you see a company with high P/E it means investors are expecting it to grow at very high levels, and if you see a company with low P/E, either its growth is expected to be very slow or investors view it as a risky bet. Another way to use P/E ratio is to compare companies within a peer group, and those with lower P/E ratios can be viewed as "relatively cheaper" and thus good target to buy. In the US, long-term historical average of P/E ratio of companies is around 14 - 16.

Earnings Yield: It is the inverse of P/E ratio, and measures how much a company is earning (EPS) as compared to the Price being paid by investors. In other words, how much each dollar of Price paid by investors is yielding in terms of Earnings.

$$Earnings\ Yield = EPS\ /\ Stock\ Price$$

Just like P/E, it can be used to compare different companies. A company with higher Earnings Yield is considered better compared to others in the same peer group.

This metric is similar to some other metrics like ROE (Return on Equity) and ROI (Return on Investments). All of these use Net Income or Earnings but the denominator is different. Both ROI and ROE use Balance Sheet or Book value based metrics like Book Value of Equity or Book Value of Invested Capital, whereas Earnings Yield is based upon the stock price – which is the current market value of company's equity. The problem with the Balance Sheet metrics is that they are calculated at their original book value and are not adjusted with time and do not reflect their current value.

Price to Sales Ratio (P/S): There are many cases, especially where earnings are highly volatile or in some cases negative, where it is hard to use P/E. In such cases, it is preferred to use P/S ratio. However, it should be used very carefully as if the compared companies have different Profit Margins, then this could lead to wrong conclusions.

<u>Price to Book Value Ratio (P/B):</u> This ratio measures current Market Value of the company (Current Stock Price multiplied by number of shares outstanding) relative to its Book Value (which is same as Owner's equity in the Balance Sheet). This is mostly used in capital intensive industries where book value provides some meaningful information. Investors also use this measure to determine how much value they will be able to salvage in case the company goes bankrupt.

MARKETING

Introduction
Marketing is a core function of most businesses, and covers a broad range from conceptualizing a product to details about how to deliver the product and its pricing, and communicating & promoting the value of the products to the consumers.

Topics in Brief
Here are the main functions within Marketing that most businesses implement and use:

Marketing Research: This is the function that focuses on gathering information about customer needs, preferences and behavior. It results in many critical decisions which can have huge impact on a firm.

Company & Competition (SWOT Analysis): Strategic analysis that analyses in detail various aspects of Strengths, Weaknesses, Opportunities, and Threats for the Company as well as its Competitors.

STP (Segmentation, Targeting, and Positioning): This relates to how the company uses its marketing strategy to meet the needs of various customer types. As the name implies, it focuses on segmenting the marketing into various groups, then identify some key segments for targeting, and focuses on how to position the product for the targeted customers.

4 P's of Marketing (Marketing Mix): Marketing Mix is the tool that helps implement the company's positioning strategy. There are four main elements in this mix, and decision about each is made keeping in mind the overall positioning strategy for the product/service. The 4 P's are: Product, Price, Placement, and Promotion.

Product Life Cycle: It is important to understand that no product lasts forever, and all products go through a complete lifecycle with each stage showing different characteristics. The four main stages of a product lifecycle are: Introduction, Growth, Maturity, and Decline.

Marketing Research
This is the function within Marketing that focuses on gathering information about the customer needs, preferences and behavior. This function is crucial to

the success of the business as many critical decisions which can have a huge impact on the company are taken based upon the Marketing Research information.

Marketing Research tries to find answers to some prominent business questions like:
- How happy are the customers with current product?
- What changes are desired by the customers in the existing products?
- How much will the customers accept a new product idea or concept?
- What price are the customers willing to pay for a new product?
- How will any changes in products, pricing or advertising affect the customer attitude and behavior?
- Which marketing/ advertising programs resonate well with the customers and which don't?

Based upon the information gathered, many important decisions are taken, including:
- Launching of new products in various market segments

- Making upgrades or changes to the existing products
- Pricing of new products and changing prices for existing products
- Advertising, branding, and promotions strategy

Another aspect of Marketing Research is that different customers may have different answers to the same question. This allows marketers to segment the Market based upon various criteria like age, sex, education, geography, social, income, interests etc. and come up with different strategies for different segments.

Methodology: Here are some of the popular methods to conduct Market Research. Most of the times, a combination of all of these is used.
- Quantitative marketing research (surveys and questionnaires)
- Qualitative marketing research (focus groups and personal interviews)
- Observation (observing customer behavior in their natural setting environment)
- Experimental (field trials)

Company & Competition (SWOT Analysis)

To make better decisions regarding selecting different products, entering new market segments, and making other strategic decisions, it is important to understand in detail various aspects of Strengths, Weaknesses, Opportunities, and Threats for the Company as well as its Competitors. This is usually done in shape of a matrix, as shown below.

SWOT analysis allows the main positives and negatives, both for the company as well as the competitors, to be seen in a summary form and helps senior management understand the overall situation much better. This analysis can be done at a broad company level as well as at an individual product level.

Strengths	Weaknesses
Advantages that a company enjoys over its competitors. Examples are strong brand loyalty, large market share, unique access to some materials or technology etc.	Disadvantages, especially relative to other competitors. Examples include weak cash position, low brand recognition, high costs of operations etc.
Opportunities	**Threats**
Changes in market, competitors, customer behavior etc. or even some previously undiscovered trends that allow a company to improve its business performance. For example: bad financial situation of a competitor, removal of restrictions in foreign markets, new customer shopping trends etc.	Things or events whose occurrence can be harmful to the company, like acquisition of key patents by rivals, increasing costs of supply materials, customers acceptance of substitute products, new competitor in the market, changing customer habits etc.

STP (Segmentation, Targeting, and Positioning)
This is an important aspect of Strategic Marketing, and is the key to how the company prioritizes its strategy to meet the needs of various customer types.

Segmentation: In this step, customers are divided into various groups based upon criteria like age, gender, education, income, lifestyle, interests etc. The basis for segmentation can be different for various products. The question to be asked is – What is the need to do Segmentation? Well, the answer is that not all people think alike. People have varying habits, likes/dislikes, preferences, tastes, ideology, spending habits etc. Interestingly, despite these variations, most people can be categorized into different groups or segments based upon these criteria. The key is how to form these groups and what criteria to use. This depends a lot on the type of the product or service being marketed. For example, a fashion clothing company may segment its customers based upon age and personality type, while an automobile maker may segment based upon the income, family size, working occupation etc. Here are some of the criteria for segmenting the market:

- Demographic (Age, Gender, Ethnicity, Marital Status, Family Size etc.)
- Geographic (City, State, Country, Continent or a Region like Central America, Middle East Asia etc.)
- Socio-economic (Income, Education, Occupation, Social class etc.)
- Psychographic (Personality, Personal Values, Interests, Attitudes, Life style etc.)
- Behavioral (Benefits sought, Product usage etc.)

Segmentation helps by allowing a company to group a very diverse market into some key homogeneous groups. This segmentation allows them to see its strengths, weakness, opportunities and threats in each segment and provides a chance to develop their strategy for each segment. . A company may chose to ignore the segmentation and go ahead with a single and undifferentiated marketing strategy, or chose different marketing strategies for different segments, or may choose to just focus on only a few of the segments.

Targeting: Once the Segmentation process is complete, the next step is Targeting. This step involves selecting a subset of those segments for "targeting" i.e. the segments that the company will try to sell to, and go after with its marketing efforts. Targeting is very important as every company has a limited amount of resources and it is often not practical to target the entire market, especially if the segments within the market are very diverse. So a company has to decide about which market segments represent the best allocation of its resources.

There are two main considerations while selecting a target market segment:

1) Segment Attractiveness: Companies chose how much a segment is attractive or profitable based upon the segment's size, growth potential, ability and willingness to spend etc.

2) Competition and Company's capabilities: Looking at how company's core capabilities and strengths align with the segment characteristics, and how much competition the company will face in that segment. This allows a company to assess the chances of its success in the given segment.

A segment which appears attractive from both these viewpoints is generally regarded as a prime target segment while the one with low scores on both criteria is avoided.

Positioning: Positioning is creating an image or identity of the product/service in the consumer's mind (relative to the competition). Positioning can be for a particular product or for a brand or even for the entire company. The main focus is to create a special "position" in the customer's mind as this is how the customer will view the company's products relative to the other competitors when they make their buying decisions.

To help with Positioning, companies first utilize some of the concepts that we have already discussed before. Segmentation and Targeting steps help create homogeneous groups, with each group potentially requiring different Positioning strategy. Marketing Research helps in getting to understand these Segments in much more detail including their needs, desires and perception of the current products in the market. Then the company decides what impression or image it wants to create in the consumer's mind to be successful in selling its products or services, and selects the appropriate advertisement and promotional campaigns to create that image.

4 P's of Marketing (Marketing Mix)

Marketing Mix is the tool that helps implement the positioning strategy. There are four main elements in this mix, and decision about each is made keeping in mind the overall positioning strategy for the product/service. For example, if a company decides to position a product as a very high class product for the very affluent folks, then it should have the top notch quality features, priced very high, offered exclusively in the very high end stores and advertising also should reflect its high end nature. The four Marketing Mix elements are:

Product: This is regarding the decision about the product attributes like key features, design, technology, internal components, quality of the product, external looks (including dimensions/size, weight, color, material etc.). Product characteristics should match with the positioning strategy. For example a company which has students as target segment will be ill advised to have a formal and expensive clothing line, while a company targeting rich gentry should not come out with a cheap car with low quality specifications.

Price: This is a very important element and its importance is not only in the marketing context as it contains elements of overall company strategy as well as financial implications. There are three main considerations while selecting a product's price:
1) Positioning Strategy: If a company wants to establish its product as a premium product, it goes for a higher price point relative to the other products in the market. This is also known as "price skimming". If the company wants to generate very high sales volumes and wants to appeal to mass markets and attract many new customers, it can go with lower price than the others. This is also known as "penetration pricing". So a company should keep its pricing in line with its overall strategy.
2): Competition: How a company prices its products is often limited by the price that the competitors are selling their products. Even if a company decides to go for price skimming or penetration pricing, it is still relative to the competition. Unless it is a whole new product category, competitive pricing usually limits the pricing range.

3) Profitability and Price Elasticity: Pricing directly impacts profitability, especially due to Price Elasticity. At higher prices, the profit per product is higher but fewer products are sold. On the other hand, if price is kept lower, the company will be able to sell a larger number of units but profit per product will be lower. So the company has to do a very detailed price elasticity analysis to figure out what pricing level results in the most optimum profitability.

Placement: This involves decisions regarding product placement i.e. the channels through which the product is distributed and sold. Again keeping in mind the overall positioning strategy, a marketing manager needs to decide which combination of retail outlets, direct sales, directly online, catalogue sales, sales force, online retailers etc. to use for selling the product. Then within each category, they need to decide which particular partners to use and which not to use. There are other decisions that also need to be made like exclusivity at certain sales partners, shelf space and shelf placement at retail stores etc.

Promotion: This element involves decisions regarding how to promote the product/service and how to get the marketing message to the target customers. It includes deciding which mediums to use for promotional campaigns such as TV/Radio ads, Newspaper/Magazine advertising, Flyers, Sponsored Events, Direct Marketing, email marketing, online marketing (Banner, Search, Social Media), PR etc. As most of the time multiple mediums are used, a big decision is regarding how much to spend on each medium. Also, another decision is regarding where to do promotions and at what time. This depends a lot on the targeted customer segments.

Product Life Cycle

It is important to understand that no product lasts forever, and all products go through a complete lifecycle with each stage showing different characteristics. The following diagram sums up the complete lifecycle of a product:

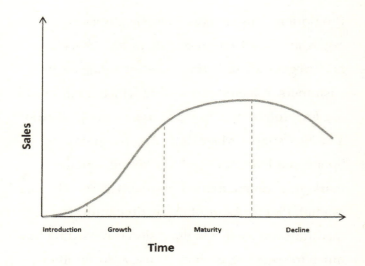

There are four unique stages in a product lifecycle:

1) Introduction: This is the earliest stage of a product when it is just introduced in the market for selling. There are very few sales, with most of the buying done by early adopters. Companies mostly tend to keep their prices high in this stage. Profits are very low or negative in this stage. This stage is also marked by high promotional expenditures. But this expenditure helps in the long term as customers associate the product and brand with this new category and it gets the first movers advantage.

2) Growth: This is the stage when the product experiences a rapid growth with high market acceptance, improved profitability and expansion of market, but also sees the arrival of competitors. This stage is also marked by increased distribution coverage and reduction in pricing due to competition as well to attract more customers. Companies focus on adding new features to the product as well as make improvements to the orginal one. Heavy promotions and marketing continues, although at reduced pace from the Introduction stage. Main focus of the companies is to increase their market share as much as possible.

3) Maturity: At some time, the growth rate starts to slow down, and this is when the product reaches its maturity stage. The product has reached most of the market and is accepted as a fully mature product by the mass market. Now there are many competitors in the market. This stage is also market by price competition as the manufacturing costs have become low and product is highly profitable due to economies of scale.

4) Decline: After the Maturity stage, the product enters its final stage of Decline when the growth becomes negative, i.e. sales start declining. Due to low sales and limited opportunity for future growth, companies start reducing their expenditures and harvest as much profitability as they can. Sometimes it can also mean aggressive price wars as companies strive to stay alive. Some companies start to withdraw out of the market.

Product Extension Strategies: As the product moves into the maturity and decline stages, some companies try to revive its growth by using product extension. This includes making extensive changes to the product and offering it as a different product or a new product extension. For example, some people consider Laptops to be a product extension of the Desktops.

STRATEGIC MANAGEMENT

Introduction

What is Business Strategy? It is a set of very high level decisions relating to the overall mission, objectives, and direction of the company as well as how to achieve them. These decisions are usually taken keeping in mind company's core strengths, overall dynamics of the industry and various players in it, competitor's strengths and weaknesses, market/customer behavior etc.

Every company has its own strategy, but there are few strategy frameworks that are used by almost everyone that helps them decide their strategy. In the following sections, we will discuss some of the most common and popular strategy frameworks.

Topics in Brief

Porter's Five Forces: This framework is used to analyze competitive forces within an industry with the end goal of determining if it makes sense for a company to enter a particular industry or not. It also allows understanding the root causes behind an industry's current structure and profitability.

Competitive Advantage and Generic Strategies: This describes how a firm can obtain sustainable competitive advantage over other firms in the same industry. There are two main types of competitive advantages: Cost leadership and Differentiation. There are three "Generic Strategies" to gain Competitive Advantage: Cost Leadership, Differentiation, and Focus.

Core Competencies: Core Competencies are the competitively unique sets of skills and expertise within the organization that enables it to deliver customer value, and gives it a competitive advantage over its competitors.

Horizontal/Vertical Integration: This is a very strategic topic that almost every company's top executives and the Board have to deal with. The basic idea is about how to improve the firm's competitive position in the industry through mergers & acquisitions (M&A). There are two main types of M&A activities that can be done: Horizontal Integration and Vertical Integration

BCG Matrix: This is a strategic tool that was developed by Boston Consulting Group (BCG) to help firms allocate resources between different products. This framework analyzes products on two criteria – market share and market growth rate.

Porter's Five Forces

This framework is named after Michael Porter who developed this in the late 1970's. This framework is used to analyze competitive forces within an industry with the end goal of determining if it makes sense for a company to enter a particular industry or not. It also allows understanding the root causes behind an industry's current structure and profitability.

According to Mr. Porter, there are five forces that shape competition within an industry:
1) Threat of new entrants
2) Threat of substitute products
3) Bargaining power of suppliers
4) Bargaining power of buyers
5) Rivalry among existing competitors

1) Threat of new entrants: If it is easy for new companies to enter the industry, it means that there will be more competition, which will lead to reduced profitability in the industry. Thus it is desirable to be in an industry which has high "barriers to entry" which make it difficult for others to enter that industry. Barriers can be in the form of possession of key technology, patents, large amount of capital required, access to resources, economies of scale etc.

2) Threat of substitute products: This concerns the propensity of the customers to substitute the industry product with another product outside the industry. If there are close substitute products and/or customers show a willingness to switch to alternatives, this affects the price elasticity for the industry and reduces profitability. For example, for flights over a short distance, other airlines are competitors but other modes of transportation like rail, bus, and car are viable substitutes.

3) Bargaining power of suppliers: This refers to the power of suppliers (who supply raw materials and other inputs to the company) to raise their prices. This power depends upon the supplier industry

characteristics including number of suppliers and intensity of rivalry, cost of switching to other suppliers, ease of switching to substitute products, etc. For more industry profitability, it is better to have low bargaining power of the suppliers.

4) Bargaining power of buyers: It is also preferable that the buyers of the industry products have low power to dictate the pricing terms or demand lower prices. This buyer power is dependent upon the concentration of players in that industry (buyer) i.e. if there are few big players in that buyer market, then it is easy for them to demand lower price, however if that industry is not concentrated and consists of a lot of small firms then any single customer doesn't have the size to dictate pricing terms. Other factors are the existence of substitute products and ease of switching, switching costs to competitors etc.

5) Rivalry among existing competitors: The intensity of competition within the industry also has big impact on the industry profitability. More intense competition leads to low profitability. Competitive

intensity is dependent upon a number of factors including:

- Concentration of industry i.e. if the industry consists of a few large players or many small firms – higher concentration with few large players often leads to lower intensity of competition while many small players lead to more intense competition.
- Switching costs between competitors - low switching costs increase competition.
- Fixed costs - high fixed costs mean low variable cost per unit which causes firms to become more aggressive in pricing and create more price competition.
- Exit barriers - if it is very expensive for a company to exit the market then it will fight very aggressively to remain in the market thus increasing the competition intensity.

Competitive Advantage and Generic Strategies

This is another strategy framework developed by Michael Porter. Here he describes how a firm can obtain sustainable competitive advantage over other firms in the same industry. Competitive advantage can be measure by higher profitability and comes from the firm's ability to provide the customers with same value as others at lower costs, or provide customers with higher value at similar cost levels as other competitors. "Sustainable" Competitive Advantage is the one that company can hold on to for a very long period of time and cannot be replicated by the competitors.

According to Mr. Porter, there are two main types of competitive advantages: Cost leadership and Differentiation. There are three "<u>Generic Strategies</u>" to gain Competitive Advantage:
1) Cost Leadership
2) Differentiation
3) Focus

A firm needs to choose one particular strategy based upon its own strengths and weaknesses and market/industry competitive dynamics. If a company is not strategically focused on one strategy, then there is danger of it getting "stuck in the middle" i.e. mediocre, and this does not translate into a sustainable competitive advantage.

<u>Cost Leadership Strategy:</u> This strategy calls for producing goods/services at the lowest cost in the industry. So profitability is enhanced not by higher revenue, but by lower costs. In case of severe price competition, the firm's lower costs will allow it to still have some profits while others in the industry incur losses. Please note that this strategy should not be confused with producing low quality products, instead the focus is on designing the overall organizational structure such that every part of the organization is focused on reducing overall company costs and eliminating any redundant or wasteful costs. Some of the strategic decisions that can be taken to support this cost leadership strategy are building large capacity plants that will produce higher economies of scale and lower cost per unit, lower inventory and material costs, cost efficient and most effective distribution channels, very agile and skilled procurement team to negotiate the best prices from suppliers, focus on operational efficiency etc. The organization needs to be very nimble and clever in keeping up with the changes in overall market and keep ahead of competitors in lowering its costs. A great example of this strategy is Wal-Mart.

Differentiation Strategy: In this strategy, a firm gains advantage over its rivals by providing products/services that are perceived by the customers to have superior features and attributes, and different from what the other competitors are offering. This allows the firm to charge a premium price for its products, even though costs are roughly similar to the competitors, thus making it more profitable. To make this a sustainable competitive advantage, a company must keep investing in resources that keep its products at the leading edge, and couple that with appropriate branding and marketing campaigns so that the company's brand garners a reputation for differentiated and superior products in customer's mind. A great example of the differentiation strategy is Apple.

Focus Strategy: This strategy means focusing on a narrow customer segment rather than the overall market. Thus, customer intimacy and loyalty is the key to this strategy. Within this customer focus, there are two strategies: Cost focus, and Differentiation Focus.

For Cost Focus strategy, a product is altered such that it fits the need of a specific segment but at a lower cost.

In Differentiation Focus strategy, special attention is given to the specific needs of that narrow market segment and products are delivered that exactly match those needs. Because of the narrow size of the market, other competitors who are focused on the overall market don't typically bother to change their products as that would mean higher costs for them as there are many narrow segments within the market and it is hard for them to meet the specific needs of them all. Since the differentiation focus leads to highly customized products, customers are willing to pay the premium price in order to get their exact demands fulfilled.

Core Competencies

This concept was developed by C.K. Prahalad and Gary Hamel. Core Competencies are the competitively unique sets of skills and expertise within the organization that enables it to deliver customer value, and gives it a competitive advantage over its competitors. Please note that core competencies are skill sets and not assets like products or machinery etc.

A fundamental thinking behind this concept is that the markets, products, and customer needs keep changing over time and trying to have a strategy based upon these can't last long, but core competencies within the organization are a fundamental source of competitive advantage that can adapt to changing times. Since competencies are the main source of competitive advantage, a firm should organize itself as a portfolio of core competencies.

There are three tests a competency must pass to be considered as a core competency:
1) Value Creation: A core competency should create a significant value for the customers.
2) Competitively Unique: A core competency must be unique to the company i.e. it should be extremely difficult for the competitors to copy.
3) Wide Use: It must be able to be used widely in the creation of many products and services, and provide access to a wide variety of markets.

Horizontal/Vertical Integration

This is a very strategic topic that almost every company's top executives and the Board have to deal with. The basic idea is about how to improve the firm's competitive position in the industry through mergers & acquisitions (M&A). There are two main types of M&A activities that can be done: Horizontal Integration and Vertical Integration.

Horizontal Integration: In this type of integration, a company decides to merge with or acquire another company that is in the same business. Most of the times, the other company is a competitor in the same industry. The main reasons for this type of integration are to get more market share and broader access to the market (economies of scale), and to get economies of scale due to larger production from the combined company. This also provides more power to the company in its negotiation with the suppliers. Also, some of the redundant operating expenses like administration and other general expenses can be reduced. For example, Hewlett-Packard buying Compaq in 2001 was an example of Horizontal Integration.

However, a lot of time the envisioned operating synergies do not actually take place. Many times the companies underestimate how hard it is to integrate two different company cultures into one coherent company direction and this often leads to chaos and consumes lot of valuable management time and energy.

Vertical Integration: In this type of integration, a company takes a look at the entire value chain across its industry, right from raw materials suppliers to the end retailers, and looks to merge with or acquire a company that performs different activity in the supply chain. For example, a manufacturing company buying a component supplier or other raw material supplier is a type of vertical integration (backward vertical integration). A software maker (like Google or Microsoft) buying a hardware company (like a PC maker or a phone maker like Motorola) is an example of Vertical Integration (forward).

The biggest rationale behind vertical integration is getting control over the value chain. Also, a company may buy very strategic technology so that it will stop being available to the competitors. Another advantage is that it provides better coo-ordination and helps improve the quality of end products, as well as speed of production. This also helps the company build barriers to entry into the industry for potential new competitors. Cost is another advantage as now the profit margins of the acquired company is retained within the combined firm.

However, one big disadvantage is that it jeopardizes relationships with the other players in the value chain who were doing the same activities as the acquired company i.e. acquired company's competitors. Before the merger/acquisition, those companies were partners (either as suppliers or distributors). Now they become the competitors. Another disadvantage, like in horizontal integration, is that it seems easier on paper but very hard to implement the actual merger of two companies with different locations, different work cultures and different mindsets.

BCG Matrix

This is a strategic tool that was developed by Boston Consulting Group (BCG) to help firms allocate resources between different products. This framework analyzes products on two criteria – market share and market growth rate. That's why it is also sometimes known as Growth-Share matrix. Market share refers to the current market share of the product being analyzed, and market growth is the growth rate of the overall market in which the product competes.

There are two main assumptions behind this tool, and some have questioned the complete validity of these assumptions. The assumptions are that high market share results in higher profitability, and high market growth rate means the product require more investments.

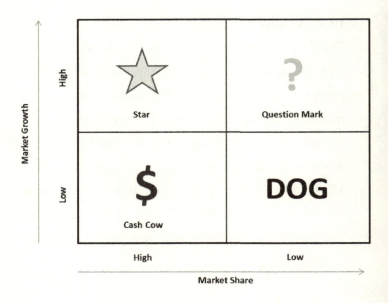

Dogs: These are the products that have low market share and this product market has low growth overall. These products burn cash as they bring in less revenues and have much higher expenses. Businesses should get rid of these products.

Cash Cows: These products have high market share and the overall market growth rate is low i.e. the market is mature. Because of high market share, these products are highly profitable, and as the market growth rate is low, the company doesn't need to make a lot of investments. So overall these products generate a lot of cash for the company.

Stars: These are the products which enjoy a high market share, and where the market growth is also high. These products generate large amount of revenue and profits, however large amount of investments also need to be made due to high growth rates. Hope is that when the market matures, these products will turn into cash cows and generate a lot of cash for the company.

Question Marks: These are the products which have low market share in a market growing at high rate. So these products have low profitability but high expenses. If the status quo continues, these products will keep producing losses and turn into Dogs. However, if the company keeps making investments, there is chance that these start gaining market share and turn into Stars and eventually Cash Cows. So either the company should try its best to make these products succeed or stop making any investments to at least generate some cash

Overall, the company strategy should be to get rid of Dogs, invest cash generated from Cash Cows into Stars and Question Marks, and decide which Question Marks to invest in and which ones not to.

Limitations: Main limitations of the BCG Matrix are that some consider its main two assumptions to be not completely valid, and it considers only market growth as indicator of market attractiveness (that too in a negative sense – investments), and only market share as indicator of profitability and success, while leaving out many other factors.

ORGANIZATIONAL BEHAVIOR

Introduction

Organizational Behavior deals with study of people, individual as well as groups, within an organization. From a business perspective, the end goal is to align employee's incentives with company's overall objectives and decide what organizational structure, people management systems, employee motivation methods, performance measurement tools, and incentive systems should a company use in order to get the most productivity and loyalty out of its employees.

Topics in Brief

<u>Organizational Structure:</u> Structure determines the hierarchy, decision making, and reporting responsibilities and activities. Sometimes it is also expressed as Organization Chart. There are two main types of structures: Flat and Hierarchical. Hierarchical structures further consist of three sub-types of structures: Functional, Divisional, and Matrix.

Motivation: Employees are the key resource for any organization and it is very important to keep the employees highly motivated. There are some main theories that explain the psychology behind motivation:
- Incentive Theory
- Expectancy Theory
- Equity Theory
- Herzberg's Two-Factor Theory
- Job Characteristics Model

Common Organizational Problems:
- Empire Building
- Performance Evaluations
- No due recognition by Managers

Organizational Structure

Every organization needs a structure, which determines the hierarchy, decision making, and reporting responsibilities and activities. Sometimes it is also expressed as Organization Chart. There are a few different ways an organization can be structured, and the senior management needs to choose the best one according to its business needs as well as that aligns best with its overall mission and objectives.

There are two main types of structures: Flat and Hierarchical.

Flat Structure: An organization has a flat structure when there are no middle management layers between employees and senior management. Such a structure is most often seen in smaller companies as it is very hard to maintain this kind of structure in large organizations. In larger companies, one may see flat structures within individual departments.

The advantages of a flat organization are that decision making is quicker, information flow is faster, and employees feel more empowered and are more motivated.

Hierarchical Structures: These structures are the ones that we see normally in most large companies, and even governments. Employees (non-managers) report to their immediate manager or supervisor, those managers report to a senior manager, and so on until there is only one head of the organization, typically the company's CEO. Looking at top down, CEO has just a few very high level senior managers (typically called Senior or Executive Vice Presidents) reporting to him, these Senior VPs have many VPs reporting to each of them, and it continues down the stack until the first level Managers have non-management employees reporting to them.

Hierarchical structures can be thought of as Pyramids, with one person at the top, and many workers at the bottom. As one goes up the pyramid, the seniority within the organization rises and the number of people at those levels keep decreasing.

There are many different ways that a hierarchical structure can be implemented. Here are some of those methods:

Functional structure: In this type of structure, the organization is divided based upon various business functions like Sales, Finance, R&D, Marketing etc. This is usually a good fit for firms that have limited number of products/services or otherwise the products/services are not too different from each other or are standardized products. This structure enables the firm to take advantage of operational efficiencies of key functional groups.

Divisional structure: Here, the organization is grouped based upon different divisions within the company, with each division containing all the necessary functional and support groups within it. The divisions can be based upon Products (also known as Product structure), Markets (like Consumer, Commercial, Kids, Youth etc.), and Geography (USA, International, Europe, Asia etc.)

Matrix structure: This is a structure using both Functional and Divisional groupings. At high level, there are both Functional and Divisional groups. As the structure moves down, there are teams that report to both the Functional and Divisional managers.

Motivation

Needless to say, one of the biggest challenges of an organization is to keep its employees highly motivated. Employees are the key resource for any organization and are often the main differentiation between good and great companies. Below are some of the key theories that explain the psychology behind motivation:

Incentive Theory: According to this theory, external rewards or incentives motivate people to do things. If rewards are presented after the right action has been performed, it will incentivize the person to perform the same action again, in order to be awarded again. Thus, the right incentive after the right action can lead to a repetition of that behavior.

Expectancy Theory: Developed by Victor Vroom in 1964, this theory explains how a person chooses a particular behavioral alternative or option over the other ones. There are three main variables in this theory: Expectancy, Instrumentality, and Valence.

Expectancy: This is the belief that better effort will result in better performance.
Instrumentality: Belief that good performance will result in good reward.
Valence: The value that the individual places on the rewards received.

Motivational Force = Expectancy * Instrumentality * Valence

Equity Theory: Developed in 1963 by John Stacey Adams, this theory asserts that a key motivational factor for employees is the sense of equity or fairness. Equity is measured by comparing the ratio of Outcomes (Rewards, Compensation etc.) to Job Inputs (Hard Work, Effort, Knowledge, Intelligence, Time etc.) for oneself to the others in the organization (peers or also could be for other workers at different levels). If this ratio is perceived to be unequal, then employees become stressed and there is tension. It happens both if they are being under-rewarded or over-rewarded. Over-rewarded feel guilt, while under-rewarded feel angry. Employees try to eliminate or relive this tension/distress by changing the input/output (for example, doing less work, finding another job etc.).

Herzberg's Two-Factor Theory: Fredrick Herzberg proposed in this theory that there are two types of motivational factors – first ones motivate employees, and the second ones don't motivate, but if absent, demotivate employees. Also, according to him salary and money are not the primary motivators, but instead the primary motivators are intrinsic factors like respect, recognition, achievement etc.

Motivational Factors: These are the factors that provide motivation to employees for a superior performance. Most of these are intrinsic factors that include respect, recognition, sense of achievement, growth opportunities, responsibilities etc.

Hygiene Factors: These are the factors that by themselves don't provide any motivation, but if absent, cause job dissatisfaction. In other words, if these factors are present, they do not make employees dissatisfied with their work. Most of these factors are extrinsic in nature and include salary, benefits, company policies, work conditions, supervision and relationship with boss, interpersonal relations with peers, job security etc.

Job Characteristics Model: According to this model, job satisfaction and employee motivation is dependent upon five key variables, and can vary from person to person, depending upon their individual attributes. The five characteristics are:
1) Skill Variety
2) Task Identity (Is the task whole or an identifiable piece of a larger task or a small/partial and hard to identify piece of much larger task)

3) Task Significance
4) Autonomy
5) Task Feedback

Common Organizational Problems
While companies try their best to implement the best practices, there are some issues that are prevalent in most of the organizations. Some of these issues that companies tend to overlook and should pay more attention to are:

Empire Building: In most of the hierarchical structures, senior managers are effectively competing with each other to reach top of the pyramid. One way of showing that they are ready for higher responsibility is by already proving themselves capable of handling wide responsibilities. This causes many senior managers to indulge in "land grabbing" and start widening the roles and responsibilities of their team. Often this is done by adding many more people to team, as one criteria used for determining the importance of a role is to consider how many people worked under a manager. This is called empire building, and often leads to wasteful hiring, redundant jobs and loss in overall productivity. But it doesn't matter to the senior managers as their primary motivation is to show off their superior management capabilities and promote themselves.

Performance Evaluations: In order to reward the right performance, first the performance needs to be measured or evaluated correctly. Thus, performance evaluation is a very integral part of the reward/incentives system. However, if not implemented correctly, this can cause serious problems and employee dissatisfaction. Some of the most common problems with Performance Evaluations are:

No Objective Metrics: Performance appraisals are often based on subjective measures and not objective metrics. It makes the whole appraisal susceptible to misinterpretation and inconsistency.

Wrong metrics: Most of the times, the metrics are same throughout the organization and it may have no or little alignment with an employee's actual work. This again leads to very inconsistent appraisals. Also, many times the metrics chosen are plain wrong. For example, a person is working in a customer support role, and one of the measures in appraisal is "visibility". Should a customer support person be focused on sitting in his/her chair and answering customer calls or going around the organization to attain more "visibility" with other managers?

Annual review cycle, no continuous feedback: More often than not, the performance appraisals are done once a year, and at most twice a year. The employees have no idea what his/her manager is thinking about his/her performance in the intervening period and comes to know only during the appraisal. Throughout the year, an employee might be focusing on one particular criterion and thinking he/she is doing a great job. But at end of the year, they find out that their manager deemed some other criteria to be more important and the resulting appraisal is not up to their satisfaction.

Forced Rankings: In many organizations a forced rankings system is used. For example, top 20% will get A rating, next 60% will get B rating, and bottom 20% will get C rating. While it is important to identify and promote the winners, this approach leads to much internal competition. Whereas the employees are supposed to work as a team and solve problems together, this approach makes them see each other as rivals and it is in their best interest to see others not succeed.

<u>No Due Recognition by Managers:</u> Another major problem in organizations is that the managers don't give due credit to their subordinates for their achievements, and even worse, take the credit themselves. In many companies, this is in fact acknowledged and accepted with the explanation being that a manager is ultimately responsible for his workers success, and that success wouldn't have been possible without the manager. It goes without saying that this is one of the worst things for employee morale. Managers should be secure in their job and not consider their direct reports as current/future competition. They should act as a guide and have the best interests of the employees in their mind. A good solution is for an employee to have frequent and direct access to a Senior Manager. That way the senior manager would be more in touch with the employee's contributions and a

manager would have to seriously think about consequences before taking undeserved credit for himself or herself.

RECOMMENDED READINGS

Economics
- The Wealth of Nations (Adam Smith)
- The General Theory of Employment, Interest and Money (John Maynard Keynes)
- Thinking Strategically (Avinash Dixit, Barry Nalebuff)

Operations
- The Goal (Eliyahu Goldratt, Jeff Cox)

Finance
- Investment Valuation (Aswath Damodaran)
- The Intelligent Investor (Benjamin Graham)
- Security Analysis (Benjamin Graham, David Dodd)
- Behavioral Investing (James Montier)

Marketing
- Marketing Management (Philip Kotler, Kevin Keller)
- Positioning: The Battle for Your Mind (Al Ries, Jack Trout) – <u>A Must Read</u>

Strategy
- HBR's 10 Must Reads: The Essentials
- HBR's 10 Must Reads on Strategy
- Competitive Strategy (Michael Porter)
- Competitive Advantage (Michael Porter)
- Competing for the Future (Gary Hamel, C.K. Prahalad)
- The Innovators Dilemma (Clayton Christensen)

General Management / Organizational Behavior
- The One Minute Manager (Kenneth Blanchard, Spencer Johnson)
- Getting to Yes (Roger Fisher, William Ury, Bruce Patton)
- HBR's 10 Must Reads on Leadership
- The Effective Executive (Peter Drucker)

Made in the USA
Las Vegas, NV
09 August 2024